Expand and Enrich
READING

Grades K-2

Annie Weissman

LINWORTH
LEARNING

From the Minds of Teachers

Linworth Publishing, Inc.
Worthington, Ohio

Expand and Enrich
READING
Grades K-2

Library of Congress Cataloging-in-Publication Data

Weissman, Annie, 1948-
    Expand and enrich reading, grades K-2 / Annie Weissman.
        p. cm.
    Includes bibliographical references.
    ISBN 1-58683-139-9 (pbk.)
    1. Reading (Primary)--United States. 2. English language--Composition
and exercises--Study and teaching (Primary)--United States. 3.
Storytelling--United States. 4. School children--Books and
reading--United States. I. Title.

    LB1525.W52 2003
    372.4--dc21

                                                                2003005192

Published by Linworth Publishing, Inc.
480 East Wilson Bridge Road, Suite L
Worthington, Ohio 43085

Author: Annie Weissman
Editor: Cindy Barden
Design and Production: Good Neighbor Press, Inc., Grand Junction, CO

ISBN: 1-58683-139-9

5 4 3 2 1

Table of Contents

Folk Tales

Fantasy

Historical Fiction

Nonfiction

Enriching Storytime

In *The Read Aloud Handbook* (Penguin, 1995) Jim Trelease states that extensive research has proven that reading aloud to a child is the single most important factor in raising a reader. He asserts that reading aloud conditions children to associate reading with pleasure. It creates background knowledge, which is important for vocabulary development, increases understanding of subjects, and compares new information with stored knowledge.

In *The Power of Reading* (Libraries Unlimited, 1993) Stephen Krashen states that when teachers read and discuss books with students, students read more.

According to Ruth Sawyer (*The Way of the Storyteller*, Viking, 1942, 1962) storytime can develop children's senses of curiosity and humor and widen their reading interests. Reading aloud allows children to enjoy books that they can understand, but which are too difficult for them to read independently.

> *Reading aloud to children is the single most important factor in raising a reader.*

Reading aloud develops children's interests and widens and varies their experiences. It acquaints children with the formal language of books and broadens their vocabulary. Reading aloud can give children a taste for good literature as well as introduce them to different genres.

This book provides suggestions for teachers and home schoolers to extend storytime into reading and writing activities with specific learning objectives that meet NCTE Standards, helping to make the enthusiastic sharing of books and stories with students an integral part of the reading and writing curriculum.

Activities in this book are divided into categories: Elements of fiction, Caldecott books, folk tales, fantasy, historical fiction, and nonfiction. Each section includes activities, reproducibles, and a related bibliography.

Elements of Fiction

One of the best ways to present literary elements is by using storytime picture books, even with students in higher grades. The advantage is that picture books can be read in a short period of time after a concept is introduced.

The first section of this book provides a basis for understanding the elements of fiction which can be applied to activities in the rest of the book. Exploring characters, setting, plot, main idea, theme, and point of view independently will enable students to grasp the whole picture and apply what they've learned to specific genres.

Activities in this section include listening to stories, writing, drawing, comparing and contrasting characters, presenting a short play, and retelling a story from a different point of view.

Caldecott Books

Caldecott medal and honor books are excellent vehicles for teaching students a variety of writing skills. These books represent diverse cultures as well as the best in children's literature.

These resources may be helpful for incorporating Caldecott books into other content units:

> Shan Glandon's *Caldecott Connections to Language Arts, Caldecott Connections to Science, Caldecott Connections to Social Studies,* (Libraries Unlimited, 2000)

> Newbery and Caldecott Awards: *A Guide to the Medal and Honor Books* (American Library Association, 2000)

More information about the Caldecott Award can be found at this Web site: http://www.ala.org/alsc/caldecott.html

Activities in this section include listening to stories, comparing different styles of art, designing a book award, writing a picture from a story, creating a story without words, and presenting a puppet show.

Folk Tales

Many folk tales have been handed down as songs and stories. They often include an element of magic or the supernatural. The main character of a folk tale is usually required to perform specific tasks or complete a quest. Folk tales often include a "villain" who tries to prevent the main character from being successful.

Some folk tales explain elements of nature such as how the world was created, why we have seasons, or why the sun moves across the sky.

Folk tales often point out human shortcomings and teach a lesson. Usually, good triumphs and is rewarded; evil is punished.

In this section, students listen to folk tales from different countries, find the countries on a world map or globe, illustrate a repetitive tale, and present a puppet show based on a folk tale.

Fantasy

Fantasy often deals with magic and the supernatural. The setting may be a world very unlike our own. Although there is no need to explain how this world came to be, once the place or situation has been created, the characters and events must be logical.

A good reference for teaching fantasy is *Bringing Fantasy Alive for Children and Young Adults* by Tim Wadham and Rachel Wadham (Linworth, 1999).

Many of the books and stories for young children are animal fantasies such as *The Runaway Bunny* by Margaret Wise Brown (Harper, 1972, 1942).

One of the most popular type of fantasy is the ghost story. Even the youngest children enjoy the surprise in *The Dark, Dark Room and Other Scary Tales* by Alvin Schwartz (HarperCollins, 1984).

Students listen to fantasy stories, compare an animal character in a fantasy to a real animal, and create their own fantasy characters and settings.

Historical Fiction

Historical fiction is set in the past. The focus is on the character or the period. Although students may not have the historical background to judge whether the period is portrayed accurately, they can observe everyday life as presented and compare it with their lives today.

Students listen to historical fiction stories, compare aspects of their lives to when their parents or grandparents were young, and take a trip through time to the California gold rush.

Other Genres

Besides folk and fairy tales, fantasy, and historical fiction, many excellent books in other genres are available for young students.

Student activities modeled on the ones in this book can be easily prepared for other types of literature.

Contemporary Realism: This genre reflects events that could happen now. By comparing their lives with those of the characters, students can gain insights into their own problems.

Common themes in contemporary fiction include belonging, loving and being loved, the need for competence, family relationships, peer relationships, and the importance of friendship. They may deal with serious contemporary problems including child abuse, death, and divorce.

Mysteries: Mysteries help students understand the need for presenting material in sequential order. The author introduces the crime or puzzle at the beginning. The main character is usually an investigator who has a motive for solving the mystery.

Readers are introduced to suspects as the investigator gathers clues and searches for a solution. A good mystery does not withhold necessary information from the reader. The reader must know what the detective knows. The characters and plot cannot be manipulated to fit the solution. It must be logical.

The mystery ends when the crime or puzzle is solved. The conflict comes from the unsolved crime and the search for answers.

Science Fiction: Science fiction has some basis in scientific fact, although it may be speculative science and may involve gadgets that are not currently available. Characters usually live in conditions that differ greatly from those we know. The conflict often arises from how people react and live under these new conditions or are affected by the scientific advances.

A short bibliography of appropriate contemporary realism, science fiction, and mystery books can be found at the end of this book.

Nonfiction

Nonfiction provides students with the ability to process and evaluate information. Much of what students write as they continue to develop their writing skills will include news articles, reports, essays, editorials, and other types of nonfiction.

Students differentiate between facts and fiction, compare and contrast a real animal with an animal in a fantasy story, and use nonfiction books to write a brief report about an animal.

Expanding Storytime to Meet the Standards

With all the time demands faced by teachers and home schoolers, and the need to provide meaningful curriculum that meets specific standards, educators have a critical need for ideas and activities that expand storytime into other areas of the curriculum.

The extensive bibliographies for each section in this book can be a welcome time-saver for the busy teacher or home schooler.

Activities are designed for kindergarten through grade two students and include

- ★ objectives and NCTE standards for each activity
- ★ specific book titles related to the activities
- ★ a list of materials for each activity
- ★ specific preparation instructions (if needed)
- ★ discussion questions
- ★ reproducible activities
- ★ skits, plays, and puppet shows students can perform

Most activities require a minimum of preparation time and materials normally found in a classroom.

Reproducible activities can be completed as a group or by individual students, depending on students' reading and writing abilities.

The discussion sections include many thought-provoking, open-ended questions and encourages students to develop vital critical and creative thinking skills.

Meeting the NCTE Standards

The NCTE Standards for Language Arts are designed to allow students the opportunities and resources to develop the language skills needed to pursue life goals and to participate fully as informed, productive members of society. The standards encourage the development of curriculum and instruction to expand students' literary abilities.

Although 12 specific standards are listed, in many cases they are not distinct and separable items, but rather a part of the whole picture of literacy development.

Standard 1

Students read a wide range of print and non-print texts to build an understanding of texts, of themselves, and of the cultures of the United States and the world; to acquire new information; to respond to the needs and demands of society and the workplace; and for personal fulfillment. Among these texts are fiction and nonfiction, classic and contemporary works.

Standard 2

Students read a wide range of literature from many periods in many genres to build an understanding of the many dimensions of human experience.

Standard 3

Students apply a wide range of strategies to comprehend, interpret, evaluate, and appreciate texts. They draw on their prior experience, their interactions with other readers and writers, their knowledge of word meaning and of other texts, their word identification strategies, and their understanding of textual features.

Standard 4

Students adjust their use of spoken, written, and visual language to communicate effectively with a variety of audiences and for different purposes.

Standard 5

Students employ a wide range of strategies as they write and use different writing process elements appropriately to communicate with different audiences for a variety of purposes.

Standard 6

Students apply knowledge of language structure, language conventions, media techniques, figurative language, and genre to create, critique, and discuss print and non-print texts.

Standard 7

Students conduct research on issues and interests by generating ideas and questions, and by posing problems. They gather, evaluate, and synthesize data from a variety of sources to communicate their discoveries in ways that suit their purpose and audience.

Standard 8

Students use a variety of technological and information resources to gather and synthesize information and to create and communicate knowledge.

Standard 9

Students develop an understanding of and respect for diversity in language use, patterns, and dialects across cultures, ethnic groups, geographic regions, and social roles.

Standard 10

Students whose first language is not English make use of their first language to develop competency in the English language arts and to develop understanding of content across the curriculum.

Standard 11

Students participate as knowledgeable, reflective, creative, and critical members of a variety of literacy communities.

Standard 12

Students use spoken, written, and visual language to accomplish their own purposes.

Elements of Fiction

Identifying Main Characters

★ **Objective:**

Students will identify and describe the main character in several stories using specific criteria.

★ **Materials:**

- ★ Several books students have read and enjoyed
- ★ Crayons and drawing paper

★ **Discussion:**

All books and stories have at least one character. The **main character** is the most important one in a story.

Characters can be people, animals (like Wilbur in *Charlotte's Web*) or nonliving objects like the teapot and cup in the movie, *Beauty and the Beast*.

Who is the main character in . . .
(One at a time, hold up several books.)

Can you name a story where the main character is an animal?

Can you name a story where the main character is something besides a person or animal?

Select one book students know well and hold it up.

What does the main character look like?

What does the character say that tells us more about himself (or herself)?

What do the character's actions tell us about the kind of person he (or she) is?

What do we learn about the main character from what other characters in the book say about him (or her)?

What does the author tell you about the main character?

★ **Activity:**

After the discussion, ask students to draw pictures of their favorite characters from any book, story, or movie.

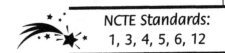

Describing Main Characters

⭐ Objective:

Students will describe the main character in *Lilly's Purple Plastic Purse* using specific criteria.

⭐ Materials:

★ *Lilly's Purple Plastic Purse* by Kevin Henkes

★ Copy of the reproducible "What They Said" for each student

★ Pencils and crayons

⭐ Activity:

Read the book to the group.

Write the following headings on the board.

How Lilly looks:

What Lilly said:

What Lilly did:

What others said about Lilly:

What the author said about Lilly:

Have students brainstorm for ideas for each heading. Write their responses. Let students refer back to the book if needed.

Give each student a copy of the speech balloon reproducible.

Help them write words or phrases in the three speech balloons.

On the back of the page, ask students to draw an action picture of Lilly that tells something important about her character.

Reinforcement: Repeat this activity using the reproducible for other stories you read to the group. Older students may be able to fill in the reproducible alone after completing the activity the first time as part of a group.

⭐ Looking Ahead:

Create a bulletin board display titled "Elements of Stories." Divide it into sections with subheadings: Characters, Setting, Plot, Theme, and Point of View. As students complete activities, display several examples of student work in the appropriate sections.

What They Said

What the main character said.

What the author said about the main character.

What someone else said about the main character.

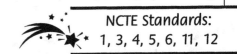

Frog and Toad

✷ Objective:

Students will compare the two main characters in *Frog and Toad Are Friends*.

✷ Materials:

- ★ *Frog and Toad Are Friends* by Arnold Lobel
- ★ One copy of the "Frog and Toad" reproducible for each student
- ★ Pencils

✷ Discussion:

How are you and one of your friends alike?

How are you and one of your friends different?

Frog and Toad are very good friends. They like to do many of the same things. But Frog and Toad are also very different.

Frog and Toad are both main characters in several books.

As you listen to the stories about Frog and Toad, think about ways they are alike and ways they are different.

✷ Activity:

Read *Frog and Toad Are Friends* to the group.

Give each student a copy of the Frog and Toad reproducible.

Complete the page as a group with younger students. Pre-reading students could also draw pictures of each character rather than write.

Older students can complete the activity alone or with a partner.

Students who enjoyed *Frog and Toad Are Friends* may also enjoy these other Frog and Toad books by Arnold Lobel:

Frog and Toad All Year

Frog and Toad Together

Days with Frog and Toad

Name _____   Date _____

Frog

Toad

Books That Emphasize Characters

Allard, Harry, *Miss Nelson Is Missing.* Houghton Mifflin, 1977.

DeGroat, Diane, *Roses Are Pink, Your Feet Really Stink.* Morrow, 1996.

De Paola, Tomie, *Strega Nona.* Prentice Hall, 1975.

Gantos, Jack, *Rotten Ralph's Rotten Romance.* Houghton Mifflin, 1997.

Goble, Paul, *The Girl Who Loved Wild Horses.* Simon & Schuster, 1983.

Graves, Keith, *Frank Was a Monster Who Wanted to Dance.* Chronicle, 1999.

Greenfield, Eloise, *She Come Bringing Me That Little Baby Girl.* HarperCollins, 1993.

Henkes, Kevin, *Chrysanthemum.* Greenwillow, 1991.

Henkes, Kevin, *Julius, the Baby of the World.* Greenwillow, 1990.

Henkes, Kevin, *Lilly's Purple Plastic Purse.* Greenwillow, 1996.

Hoban, Lillian, *Arthur's Great Big Valentine.* HarperCollins, 1989.

Hoban, Russell, *Bread and Jam for Frances.* HarperCollins, 1964.

Hoffman, Mary, *Amazing Grace.* Dial, 1991.

Kraus, Robert, *Leo the Late Bloomer.* Simon & Schuster, 1971.

Lester, Helen, *Tacky the Penguin.* Houghton Mifflin, 1988.

Lionni, Leo, *Frederick.* Knopf, 1987.

Lobel, Arnold, *Frog and Toad Together.* HarperCollins, 1971.

London, Jonathan, *Froggy Plays Soccer.* Viking, 1999.

Loredo, Elizabeth, *Boogie Bones.* Putnam, 1997.

Low, Joseph, *Mice Twice.* Atheneum, 1980.

Marshall, James, *George and Martha.* Houghton Mifflin, 1972.

Marshall, James, *The Cut-Ups.* Puffin, 1986.

McKee, David, *Elmer.* Lothrop, 1989.

McKissack, Patricia, *Flossie and the Fox.* Dial, 1986.

McPhail, David, *Pig Pig Grows Up.* Dutton, 1980.

Mora, Pat, *Tomas and the Library Lady.* Knopf, 1997.

Potter, Beatrix, *Peter Rabbit.* Little Simon, 1986.

Prigger, Mary Skillings, *Aunt Minnie McGranahan.* Clarion, 1999.

Rahaman, Vashanti, *Read for Me, Mama.* Boyds Mills, 1997.

Rey, H.A., *Curious George.* Houghton Mifflin, 1973, 1941.

San Souci, Robert D., *A Weave of Words.* Orchard, 1998.

Sendak, Maurice, *Pierre.* HarperCollins, 1990, 1962.

Shannon, George, *Lizard's Song.* Mulberry, 1992, 1981.

Soto, Gary, *Chato's Kitchen.* Putnam, 1997.

Steig, William, *Dr. De Soto.* Scholastic, 1982.

Steptoe, John, *Stevie.* Harper & Row, 1969.

Williams, Suzanne, *Library Lil.* Dial, 1997.

Elements of Fiction

Setting: When and Where?

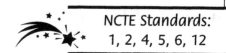
NCTE Standards:
1, 2, 4, 5, 6, 12

⭐ Objectives:

Students will relate the terms past, present, and future to the setting of a story. They will use visual clues to identify when a story takes place and write a sentence describing a setting.

⭐ Materials:

★ Copy of "When Did It Happen?" for each student
★ Pencils and crayons

⭐ Discussion:

We know that all stories have characters. We learn about characters from how they look, what they say, what they do, what other characters say, and what the author says.

Stories also have a setting. The **setting** of a story is when and where it takes place.

Stories can take place in the present, the past, or the future.

What does **past** mean?

What stories do you know that take place in the past?

What does **present** mean?

What stories do you know that take place in the present?

What does **future** mean?

What stories do you know that take place in the future?

What clues tell us **when** a story takes place?
(pictures, words—like long ago or once upon a time)

What clues tell us **where** a story takes place?

What settings for stories do you know?

⭐ Activity:

Give each student a copy of "When Did It Happen?" to complete individually or as a group.

When they finish, ask several volunteers to read their sentences.

Add copies of student work to the "Elements of Stories" bulletin board display.

When Did It Happen?

Circle *past, present,* or *future* for each setting. Color the pictures.

past   present   future

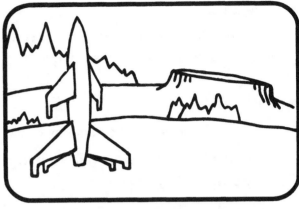

past   present   future

past   present   future

past   present   future

past   present   future

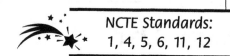

Describe a Setting

⭐ Objective:

Students will understand that the setting of a story is a vital component by predicting how a different setting would change a familiar story.

⭐ Materials:

- ★ *Lilly's Purple Plastic Purse* by Kevin Henkes
- ★ Another book listed in the bibliography for this section
- ★ Pictures of a variety of settings cut from magazines or downloaded from the Internet
- ★ Pencils and lined paper

⭐ Activity:

Read *Lilly's Purple Plastic Purse* to the group if you have not done so previously. Then continue with the discussion questions.

Does this story take place in the past, present, or future?

What clues tell you when it takes place?

What clues tell you where it takes place?

Can a story take place in more than one place?

In what two places does this story take place?

Why is the setting important to a story?

How might this story change if it took place in a different time or place?

Show students four or five pictures of various settings, one at a time.

For each picture, ask them to predict how the story would change if the setting changed.

Read another book to the group.

Have students write words and phrases to describe the setting in this book.

16

Books That Emphasize Setting

Adams, Adrienne, *A Woggle of Witches*. Scribners, 1971.

Bunting, Eve, *Train to Somewhere*. Clarion, 1996.

Bunting, Eve, *A Turkey for Thanksgiving*. Clarion, 1991.

Cannon, Janell, *Stellaluna*. Harcourt, 1993.

DeGroat, Diane, *Roses Are Pink, Your Feet Really Stink*. Morrow, 1996.

Galdone, Paul, *The Three Bears*. Clarion, 1972.

Hoban, Lillian, *Arthur's Great Big Valentine*. HarperCollins, 1989.

Hoestalandt, J., *Star of Fear, Star of Hope*. Walker, 1995.

Johnson, Paul Brett, *Lost*. Orchard, 1996.

Kimmel, Eric A., *Herschel and the Hanukkah Goblins*. Holiday House, 1989.

Lester, Julius, *Black Cowboy, Wild Horses*. Dial, 1988.

Lewin, Betsy, *What's the Matter, Habibi?* Clarion, 1997.

Lewin, Hugh, *Jafta and the Wedding*. Carolrhoda, 1983, 1981.

Lewin, Ted, *The Storytellers*. Lothrop, 1998.

London, Jonathan, *Froggy Gets Dressed*. Viking, 1992.

Martin, Jacqueline Briggs, *Snowflake Bentley*. Houghton Mifflin, 1998.

Mayer, Mercer, *Liza Lou and the Yeller Belly Swamp*. Four Winds, 1984.

McCloskey, Robert, *Make Way for Ducklings*. Viking, 1969.

McLerran, Alice, *Roxaboxen*. Lothrop, 1990.

McLerran, Alice, *The Year of the Ranch*. Viking, 1996.

McPhail, David, *Farm Morning*. Harcourt, 1985.

Moss, Marissa, *True Heart*. Silver Whistle, 1999.

Nerlove, Miriam, *Flowers on the Wall*. Margaret K. Elderberry, 1996.

Noble, Trinka Hakes, *The Day Jimmy's Boa Ate the Wash*. Dial, 1980.

Raczek, Linda Theresa, *The Night the Grandfathers Danced*. Northland, 1995.

Seuling, Barbara, *Winter Lullaby*. Harcourt, 1998.

Sharmat, Marjorie Wienman, *Gila Monsters Meet You at the Airport*. Scott Foresman, 1983.

Soto, Gary, *Too Many Tamales*. Putnam, 1996.

Stanley, Diane, *Saving Sweetness*. Putnam, 1996.

Stewart, Sarah, *The Gardener*. Farrar, 1997.

Tamar, Erika, *The Garden of Happiness*. Harcourt, 1996.

Ward, Lynd, *The Biggest Bear*. Houghton, 1988, 1952.

Wellington, Monica, *Night City*. Dutton, 1998.

Wiesner, David, *Tuesday*. Clarion, 1991.

Winch, John, *The Old Woman Who*

17

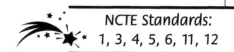

Plot: Events in Sequence

⭐ Objective:

Students will demonstrate knowledge of plot as a sequence of events by putting the main events of a story in correct order.

⭐ Materials:

- ★ *Lilly's Purple Plastic Purse* by Kevin Henkes
- ★ Another book listed in the bibliography for this section
- ★ Paper and pencils
- ★ Copy of "What I Did Today" for each student

⭐ Discussion:

Stories have characters and settings. The **setting** is when and where the story takes place.

The **plot** of a story includes the events that take place.

Would you unbutton your jacket before or after you took it off? Why?

Does it matter what order you do things, like get ready for school or bake a cake? Why?

Why is the order of events important in a story?

⭐ Activity:

Ask students to complete the reproducible, "What I Did Today."

Read *Lilly's Purple Plastic Purse* to the group if you have not done so previously.

Write these sentences on the board. As a group, number the sentences in sequential order.

Lilly draws a mean picture of Mr. Slinger.

Lilly get a new purple plastic purse.

Mr. Slinger gives Lilly her purse back.

Mr. Slinger puts Lilly's purse away.

Lilly draw a nice picture of Mr. Slinger.

Read another book to the group. Ask students to write three sentences about the story relating events in sequential order.

Add copies of student's work to the "Elements of Stories" bulletin board display.

Name _____ Date _____

What I Did Today

The first thing I did today when I got to school was

_____

_____

_____

Then, I

_____

_____

_____

Next, I

_____

_____

_____

Then, I

_____

_____

_____

Elements of Fiction

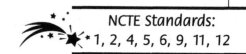

Plot: A Problem and a Solution

⭐ Objective:

Students show understanding of the concepts of problems and solutions by applying them to stories.

⭐ Materials:

★ *Too Much Noise* by Ann McGovern

⭐ Discussion:

The plot includes the events in order. The plots of most stories also include some type of problem and how the problem is solved.

What is the problem in *Lilly's Purple Plastic Purse*?

How is the problem solved?

⭐ Activity:

If students are familiar with the books, *Charlotte's Web* and *Stone Soup*, ask these questions. If not, select other titles they know well and phrase the questions accordingly.

What is the problem in *Charlotte's Web*?

How is the problem solved?

Who solves the problem?

What is the problem in *Stone Soup*?

How is the problem solved?

Read *Too Much Noise* to the group. Then ask these questions.

What is the problem in *Too Much Noise*?

What advice did the wise man give Peter?

Do his ideas work?

How is the problem solved?

Write "Advice to Peter" on the board.

Have students brainstorm for ideas to help Peter solve his problem.

Write their ideas below the heading.

When finished, students can vote on the advice they think is best.

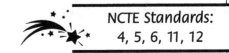

Could Anything Be Worse?

⭐ Objective:

Students will communicate with an audience by presenting an adaptation of *Too Much Noise.*

⭐ Materials:

★ One copy of the play, "Could Anything Be Worse?" for each student who will be playing a part

★ Yellow marker

★ Art materials and 11 sheets of construction paper

★ Stapler

⭐ Preparation:

1. Prepare each copy of the play by highlighting all the speaking parts for one of the characters, i.e., on one copy, highlight only the narrator's words, on another, highlight only the husband's words, etc.

2. Staple pages for each set together.

⭐ Activity:

Tell students they will be presenting a play much like the story *Too Much Noise.*

Assign each student a part in the play, "Could Anything be Worse?"

If there are more students than speaking parts, some can hold up pictures at appropriate times during the play instead.

One student can welcome the audience and announce the play and participants.

If you have too few students, some can play more than one part.

You can read the narrator portions if none of the students are able to read that well.

Give students their copies of the play.

Have them line up in the front of the room in the order characters first speak.

Could Anything Be Worse? *(continued)*

As you read through the play, have students follow on their copies.

Cue students when it is their turn to read specific parts and, if necessary, read it through with them.

Once they are familiar with the story, have students work together to draw and color one character from the play (except the narrator) on each piece of construction paper.

> Students who do not have speaking parts could be assigned to complete the artwork while other students practice their parts individually or in small groups.

Encourage students to practice reading their parts at home with parents or older siblings.

Some parts of this plan can be easily memorized by students. Others may need to read from the script.

Practice the play as a group until students are comfortable with their parts.

Those holding up pictures should know which ones to hold up when.

> If no students are assigned to hold up the pictures, tape them to the wall above the students who are playing each specific part.

Students can present the play to other classes in the library, at a school assembly, or as part of a Family Night gathering.

Could Anything Be Worse?

An old Jewish tale retold by Annie Weissman

Characters: *Narrator, Husband, Wife, Husband's Mother, Son, Daughter, Rabbi, Chickens, Rooster, Goat, Cow, Donkey*

Narrator: Once upon a time a man lived with his wife, his mother, and his children in a tiny house.

Son: Give me back my book!

Daughter: It's not your book! It's mine!

Wife: Children, stop arguing!

Husband's Mother: Why are you yelling at the children?

Husband: I can't take it any more. I'm going to see the rabbi.

Narrator: So the man went to see the rabbi.

Husband: Rabbi! I live in a tiny house with my children, my wife, and my mother. Everyone is always shouting.

Could anything be worse?

Rabbi: Hmm, let me think about this. Hmm. Do you have any chickens?

Husband: Yes, I own a few, and a rooster, too.

Rabbi: Bring them into the house to live with you.

Husband: If that will help, I'll do as you say, Rabbi.

Narrator: The man went home and brought the chickens into the house.

Chickens: Cluck! Cluck! Cluck!

Rooster: Cock-a-doodle—doo! Cock-a-doodle—doo!

Wife: There are eggs everywhere! The children are smashing them under their shoes!

Husband's Mother: What a mess!

Daughter: That rooster wakes us up too early!

Son: Ouch! A chicken pecked me!

Husband: I can't stand the noise!

Narrator: So the man went to see the rabbi.

Husband: Rabbi! My children, my wife, and my mother are still shouting and complaining!

The chickens are laying eggs everywhere, and the rooster wakes us up!

Could anything be worse?

Rabbi: Hmm, let me think about this. Hmm. Do you have any goats?

Husband: One goat.

Rabbi: Good! Take it to live inside with you.

Narrator: So the man went home and took the goat into the house.

Son: Hey, don't hit me!

Daughter: It wasn't me! The goat butted you!

Wife: No eggs for breakfast! The goat stomped on them, then licked them up!

Husband's Mother: That goat is nibbling my knitting!

Goat: Naaa! Naaa!

Chickens: Cluck! Cluck! Cluck!

Rooster: Cock-a-doodle—doo! Cock-a-doodle—doo!

Husband: I can't stand the noise and confusion!

Narrator: So the man went back to the rabbi.

Husband: Rabbi! My children, my wife, and my mother are still shouting and complaining!

The goat is eating up our food, butting the children, and nibbling on my mother's knitting! Could anything be worse?

Rabbi: Hmm, let me think about this. Hmm.

Do you have a cow?

Husband: Yes, I do, Rabbi.

Rabbi: Good! Take it to live inside with you.

Narrator: So the man went home and took the cow into the house.

Cow: Moo! Moo! Moo!

Goat: Naaa! Naaa!

Chickens: Cluck! Cluck! Cluck!

Rooster: Cock-a-doodle—doo! Cock-a-doodle—doo!

Son: That cow never stops mooing! I haven't slept in days!

Daughter: The cow's bell is driving me crazy!

Wife: That cow keeps tracking in mud!

Husband's Mother: That cow stomped on my foot!

Husband: I can't stand the noise and confusion!

Narrator: So the man went back to the rabbi.

Husband: Rabbi! My children, my wife, and my mother are still shouting and complaining!

Eggs are everywhere!

I have a bruise from where the goat butted me!

The cow is too upset to give any milk!

Could anything be worse?

Rabbi: Hmm, let me think about this. Hmm.

Do you have a donkey?

Husband: Yes, I do, Rabbi.

Rabbi: Good! Take it to live inside with you.

Husband: Are you sure about this Rabbi? Will this help me out?

Rabbi: Don't argue with me! I know good advice when I give it!

Narrator: So the man went home and took the donkey into the house.

Donkey: Hee-haw! Hee-haw! Hee-haw!

Cow: Moo! Moo! Moo!

Goat: Naaa! Naaa!

Chickens: Cluck! Cluck! Cluck!

Rooster: Cock-a-doodle—doo! Cock-a-doodle—doo!

Son and daughter: The donkey keeps kicking me!

Wife: I can't get anything done because this donkey won't get out of the way!

Husband's Mother: The goat is at my knitting again!

Husband: I can't stand the noise and confusion!

Narrator: So the man went back to the rabbi.

Husband: Rabbi! We have no milk!

The goat chewed on my books!

We can't get in the door because the donkey won't move out of the way! I had to crawl out the window to get here.

We get no sleep between the cock-a-doodle-dooing and the mooing!

Could anything be worse?

Rabbi: Hmm, let me think about this. Hmm.

Do the donkey and cow have a place to live, other than your house?

Husband: Yes, Rabbi. We have a barn.

Rabbi: Then take them out to the barn.

Does the goat have somewhere to live, other than your house?

Husband: Yes, Rabbi. We have a pen for it.

Rabbi: Good, then put the goat out in the pen.

And the chickens? Do they have a place to live, other than your house?

Husband: Yes, Rabbi, they can live in the coop with the rooster.

Rabbi: Good, then put the rooster and the chickens in the coop.

Husband: I will, Rabbi.

Narrator: So the man went home and took the donkey and cow to the barn, the goat to its pen, and the chickens and rooster to their coop.

Then he, his wife, his mother, and his children cleaned up the tiny house.

After a week, the man went back to see the rabbi.

Husband: Rabbi, how can I thank you? My life is so peaceful now!

With only my wife, my mother, and my children, our house is quite big enough! And so quiet!

Thank you so much Rabbi!

Narrator: And so things never got worse again.

Books That Emphasize Plot and Conflict

Aardema, Verna, *Borreguita and the Coyote*. Knopf, 1991.

Browne, Anthony, *The Piggybook*. Knopf, 1986.

Cole, Joanna, *Bony-Legs*. Scholastic, 1983.

Cronin, Doreen, *Click, Clack, Moo: Cows That Type*. Simon & Schuster, 2000.

Diakite, Baba Wague, *The Hatseller and the Monkeys*. Scholastic, 1999.

Everitt, Betsy, *Mean Soup*. Voyager/Harcourt, 1992.

Hazen, Barbara, *Tight Times*. Puffin, 1983.

Henkes, Kevin, *Owen*. Greenwillow, 1993.

Hest, Amy, *When Jessie Came Across the Sea*. Candlewick, 1997.

Johnston, Tony, *Alice Nizzy Nazzy, the Witch of Sante Fe*. Putnam, 1998.

Kasza, Keiko, *Wolf's Chicken Soup*. Putnam, 1996.

Keats, Ezra Jack, *Goggles*. Viking, 1998.

Kvasnosky, Laura McGee, *Zelda and Ivy*. Candlewick, 1998.

Lionni, Leo, *Swimmy*. Pantheon, 1963.

McKissack, Patricia, *Flossie and the Fox*. Dial, 1986.

Mayer, Mercer, *Liza Lou and the Yeller Belly Swamp*. Four Winds, 1984.

Meddaugh, Susan, *Hog-Eye*. Houghton Mifflin, 1995.

Ness, Evaline, *Sam Bangs and Moonshine*. Holt, 1966.

San Souci, Robert D., *The Faithful Friend*. Simon & Schuster, 1995.

Seeger, Pete, *Abiyoyo*. Simon & Schuster, 1986.

Sendak, Maurice, *Where the Wild Things Are*. HarperCollins, 1988.

Seuss, Dr., *How the Grinch Stole Christmas*. Random, 1957.

Seuss, Dr., *The Sneetches and Other Stories*. Random, 1989, 1961.

Shannon, David, *David Goes to School*. Blue Sky Press, 1999.

Shannon, David, *No, David!* Blue Sky Press, 1998.

Shannon, George, *Dance Away*. Greenwillow, 1982.

Soto, Gary, *Too Many Tamales*. Putnam, 1996.

Trivizas, Eugene, The *Three Little Wolves and the Big Bad Pig*. Margaret McElderry, 1993.

Turkle, Brinton, *Do Not Open*. Dutton, 1985.

Wells, Rosemary, *Bunny Cakes*. Dial, 1997.

Wilhelm, Hans, *Tyrone the Horrible*. Scholastic, 1988.

Williams, Vera B., *A Chair for My Mother*. Greenwillow, 1983.

Woodruff, Elvira, *The Memory Coat*. Scholastic, 1999.

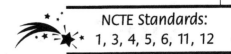

NCTE Standards:
1, 3, 4, 5, 6, 11, 12

The Main Idea

⭐ Objective:

Students will determine the main ideas of several stories.

⭐ Materials:

- ★ *Lilly's Purple Plastic Purse* by Kevin Henkes
- ★ *Too Much Noise* by Ann McGovern
- ★ Another book listed in the bibliography for this section
- ★ One copy of the "The Main Idea" for each student
- ★ Fine tip markers

⭐ Discussion:

A story has a main idea.

The **main idea** is what the story is about.

The main idea can be the lesson learned by the main character.

In *Lilly's Purple Plastic Purse*, what lesson did Lilly learn?

In *Too Much Noise*, what lesson did Peter learn?

⭐ Activity:

Read another book chosen from the bibliography for this section aloud to the students.

As a group, discuss the main idea (lesson(s) learned by the main character).

Give each student a copy of "The Main Idea" reproducible.

Ask students to write the main idea from this book on scrap paper. Encourage students to write in complete sentences.

As you help students write their sentences, notice which ones have different, but correct ideas.

Once they have good sentences written on scrap paper, they can rewrite them inside the lightbulb with fine tip markers.

Show the group two or three different sentences. Talk about how there can be more than one "right" answer.

⭐ Reinforcement:

Repeat this activity using the reproducible for other stories you read to the group.

Name _____ Date _____

The Main Idea

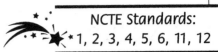

The Theme—The Idea Behind the Story

⭐ Objective:

Students will determine the theme of a story and write a "saying" based on the theme.

⭐ Materials:

- ★ *Lilly's Purple Plastic Purse* by Kevin Henkes
- ★ *Too Much Noise* by Ann McGovern
- ★ *Stone Soup* by Marcia Brown
- ★ One copy of the "soup pot" reproducible for each student
- ★ Colored pencils or markers

⭐ Discussion:

We learned that stories have characters, settings, and plots.

Stories also have themes.

The **theme** of a story is what the author wants us to think about after reading the story. It is the idea "behind" the story.

(Note: It's easy to mix up main idea and theme. Try to get across the idea that the theme includes a "universal idea" like love, friendship, cooperation, honesty, etc.)

What do you think is the theme of *Too Much Noise*?

Possible answers:

Sometimes what seems like good advice, might not be so good after all.

Maybe things aren't as bad as you think.

Things could be worse. Be happy with the way they are.

⭐ Activity:

Read *Stone Soup* by Marcia Brown to the group.

Talk about several themes for this book (sharing, co-operation, etc.).

Have them write a "saying" based on a theme from *Stone Soup* on scrap paper. (Example: If everyone shares a little, there will be enough for all.)

Give each student a copy of the soup pot reproducible. They can write their "sayings" with markers or colored pencils.

Add copies of student sayings to the "Elements of Stories" bulletin board display.

Name _____ Date _____

The Theme

Books That Emphasize Theme

Altman, Linda Jacobs, *The Legend of Freedom Hill*. Lee & Low, 2000.

Brown, Margaret Wise, *The Runaway Bunny*. Harper, 1972, 1942.

Casler, Leigh, *The Boy Who Dreamed of an Acorn*. Philomel, 1994.

Clifton, Lucille, *Everett Anderson's Friend*. Holt, 1992.

Coursen, Valerie, *Mordant's Wish*. Holt, 1997.

Demi, *The Empty Pot*. Holt, 1990.

Eduar, Gilles, *Jooka Saves the Day*. Orchard, 1997.

Egan, Tim, *Metropolitan Cow*. Houghton, 1996.

Ernst, Lisa Campbell, *Zinnia and Dot*. Viking, 1992.

Everitt, Betsy, *Mean Soup*. Harcourt, 1992.

Fine, Edith Hope, *Under the Lemon Moon*. Lee & Low Books, 1999.

Gackenback, Dick, *Claude the Dog*. Seabury, 1974.

Haas, Jesse, *Busybody Brandy*. Greenwillow, 1990.

Henkes, Kevin, *Julius, the Baby of the World*. Greenwillow, 1990.

Isadora, Rachel, *Max*. Collier, 1984, 1976.

Jackson, Isaac, *Somebody's New Pajamas*. Dial, 1996.

Johnston, Tony, *Sparky and Eddie: Wild, Wild Rodeo*. Scholastic, 1998.

Joose, Barbara, *Mama, Do You Love Me?* Chronicle, 1991.

Lewin, Hugh, *Jafta's Father*. Carolrhoda, 1983, 1981.

Lionni, Leo, *Frederick*. Knopf, 1987.

McCourt, Lisa, *I Miss You, Stinky Face*. Troll, 1999.

Mitchell, Lori, *Different Just Like Me*. Charlesbridge, 1999.

Rathmann, Peggy, *Officer Buckle and Gloria*. Putnam, 1995.

Scheffler, Ursel, *Who Has Time for Little Bear?* Doubleday, 1998.

Williams, Vera B., *A Chair for My Mother*. Greenwillow, 1983.

Yorinks, Arthur, *Hey, Al*. Farrar, 1986.

Young, Ed, *Seven Blind Mice*. Philomel, 1992.

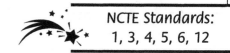

NCTE Standards:
1, 3, 4, 5, 6, 12

More Than One Point of View

⭐ Objective:

Students will identify the point of view of a story.

⭐ Materials:

★ Your favorite version of "The Gingerbread Man"

⭐ Discussion:

We learned that stories have characters, settings, plots, and themes.

Stories can also be told from different points of view.

If the **point of view** changes from one character to another, the whole story can change.

Imagine this scene: Jim is building a tower with blocks. Amy comes along and knocks down the tower.

What do you think Jim might say?

What do you think Amy might say?

Jim would have a different point of view than Amy.

⭐ Activity:

Read or tell the story of the "Gingerbread Man" to the group.

From who's point of view is the story told?

Model how the story would be different if told from a different point of view, for example, from the old woman's point of view.

"My husband and I don't have any children. One day, while I was baking gingerbread cookies, I sculpted a boy. I put two fine fat raisins for the eyes, a chocolate chip for the nose, a red hot candy for the mouth, and icing for a jacket. I put him in the oven to bake. When it was time for him to be done, I opened the oven door. Out jumped my gingerbread boy! It gave me the scare of my life! My husband and I chased him across the room, but he ran out the door. How I wanted that little gingerbread boy! He teased me by saying, 'Run, run, as fast as you can, you can't catch me, I'm the gingerbread man.'"

How are the two stories about the Gingerbread Man different?

Elements of Fiction

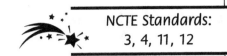

From Another Point of View

⭐ Objective:

Students will retell part of a well-known story from a different character's point of view.

⭐ Materials:

★ Your favorite version of the story of "Goldilocks and the Three Bears"

⭐ Discussion:

How do you think the story of *Lilly's Plastic Purse* would be different if it was told from Mr. Slinger's point of view?

⭐ Activity:

Read or tell the story of "Goldilocks and the Three Bears" to the group.

Ask students to think about how the story would be different if told from the point of view of the bears.

Divide the students into three groups.

Explain to the first group that they will retell the part of the story where the bears come home and discover that someone has been eating their porridge from Papa Bear's point of view.

The second group will retell the part of the story where the bears discover someone had been sitting in their chairs from Mama Bear's point of view.

The third group will tell the ending of the story from Baby Bear's point of view.

Give students time as a group to think and talk about how to tell their part of the story. Ask each group to select one person to combine the group's ideas and be the story teller.

The story tellers for each group can take turns retelling their parts of the story from the point of view of each of the three bears.

Books That Emphasize Point of View

Buchanan, Ken, *This House Is Made of Mud.* Northland, 1991.

Cohen, Miriam, *Will I Have a Friend?* Simon & Schuster, 1967.

Domanska, Janina, *Marilka.* Macmillan, 1970.

Galdone, Paul, *Little Red Hen.* Clarion, 1973.

Galdone, Paul, *The Magic Porridge Pot.* Houghton Mifflin, 1976.

Gelman, Rita Golden, *I Went to the Zoo.* Scholastic, 1993.

Graham, Bob, *Crusher is Coming.* Viking, 1988.

Greenfield, Eloise, *Me and Neesie.* Crowell, 1975.

Havill, Jaunita, *Jamaica Tag-Along.* Houghton Mifflin, 1989.

Hayes, Joe, *Soft Child: How Rattlesnake Got Its Fangs.* Roberts Rhinehart, 1993.

Hort, Lenny, *How Many Stars in the Sky?* Mulberry, 1997.

Keats, Ezra Jack, *Whistle for Willie.* Viking, 1964.

Krensky, Stephen, *My Teacher's Secret Life.* Simon & Schuster, 1996.

Kroll, Virginia, *Faraway Drums.* Little, Brown, 1998.

Lewin, Hugh, *Jafta's Mother.* Carolrhoda, 1983, 1981.

Lobel, Arnold, *On Market Street.* Greenwillow, 1981.

Marshall, James, *Yummers!* Houghton Mifflin, 1972.

McAllister, Angela, *The Snow Angel.* Lothrop, 1993.

Pinkwater, Daniel M., *I Was a Second Grade Werewolf.* Dutton, 1983.

Rylant, Cynthia, *When I Was Young in the Mountains.* Dutton, 1982.

Sceiszka, Jon, *The True Story of the Three Little Pigs.* Viking, 1989.

Trivizas, Eugene, *The Three Little Wolves and the Big Bad Pig.* Margaret McElderry, 1993.

Wood, Audrey, *King Bidgood's in the Bathtub.* Harcourt, 1985.

Yolen, Jane, *The Musicians of Bremen.* Simon & Schuster, 1996.

Bringing It All Together

☀ Objective:

Students will review the elements of fiction previously learned.

☀ Materials:

★ "Elements of Stories" bulletin board display if created

☀ Activity:

If you created an "Elements of Stories" bulletin board display, point to each item as you review that element with students.

If you did not create a display, write these words on the board: Main Character, Setting, Plot, Main Idea, Theme, Point of View. Point to each as you review that elements.

Characters can be people, animals, or nonliving things. The main character is the most important one.

We learn about **characters** from how they look, what they say, and what they do.

We also learn about **characters** from what the author and other characters say.

The **setting** of a story is when and where it takes place.

The **plot** of the story includes the events, in order.

The **plot** also includes the main problem and solution.

The **main idea** is what the story is about.

The **main idea** can be the lesson learned by the main character.

The **theme** of a story is what the author wants us to think about after reading the story. It is the idea "behind" the story.

Stories can also be told from different points of view. If the **point of view** changes, the whole story can change.

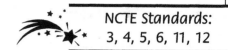

A Book About a Book

⚡ Objective:

Students will work cooperatively to prepare a book that combines the elements of fiction for a specific story.

⚡ Materials:

- ★ One storybook for each group
- ★ 10 sheets of colored construction paper, labeled as described, plus one blank sheet per group
- ★ Crayons, markers, paints, colored pencils, etc.
- ★ Stapler
- ★ Black marker
- ★ Adult leader for each group

⚡ Preparation:

1. Select one book for each group (from any of the bibliographies or some of your personal favorites).

2. Use a black marker to head 10 sheets of construction paper as shown on the following page. Leave most of the page blank for students to fill in with words and pictures.

3. Prepare one set for each group.

⚡ Activity:

Divide students into groups of three to five students. Each group should have an adult leader.

After the group leader reads the book selected for that group, he or she explains that the group will make a book about this story using what the students learned about characters, plot, setting, theme, main idea, and point of view.

The group leader shows each of the labeled pages and leads a discussion about what the students might write or draw on each page for the story they just heard.

These will be the pages for their group book.

Encourage creativity and cooperation on this project. Students can work independently or together on individual pages, but all should complete some parts of the group book.

When finished, staple the pages together to make a group book with a blank page at the end. Have each of the students write their names on this page.

Display finished books in the classroom, library, or media center.

A Book About a Book *(continued)*

Title
_____
_____

Author
_____
_____
_____

The Main Character is
_____

This is how the main character looks:

These words describe the main character:
_____
_____

What the Main Character Did
_____
_____
_____
_____
_____
_____
_____
_____

What the Main Character Said
_____
_____
_____
_____
_____

The Setting: When and Where
_____
_____
_____
_____
_____
_____

The Plot: Main Events
_____
_____
_____
_____
_____
_____
_____

The Problem

The Solution

The Main Idea
_____
_____
_____
_____
_____

The Theme
_____
_____
_____
_____
_____
_____

Point of View
👀
_____
_____
_____
_____
_____
_____

Books that Include Plays, Activities, and Patterns

Anderson, Dee, *Amazingly Easy Puppet Plays*. American Library Association, 1997, 235pp.

Anderson, Paul S., *Storytelling with the Flannel Board*. T.S. Dennison, 1963, 270pp.

Barchers, Suzanne I., *Multicultural Folktales: Readers Theatre for Elementary Students*. Libraries Unlimited, 2000, 188pp.

Gerke, Pamela, *Multicultural Plays For Children Volume 1: Grades K–3*. Smith and Kraus, 1999, 161pp.

Gerke, Pamela, *Multicultural Plays For Children Volume 2: Grades 4–6*. Smith and Kraus, 1999, 199pp.

Hicks, Doris Lynn, *Flannel Board Classic Tales*. American Library Associate, 1997, 165pp.

McCullough, L. E., *Plays from Fairy Tales*. Smith and Kraus, 1997, 183pp.

Milford, Susan, *Tales Alive! Ten Multicultural Folktales with Activities*. Williamson, 1995, 127pp.

Sierra, Judy, *The Flannel Board Storytelling Book*. H.W. Wilson, 1997, 204pp.

Sierra, Judy, *Multiculutral Folktales for the Feltboard and Readers' Theater*. Oryx, 1996, 186pp.

Sierra, Judy and Kaminski, Robert, *Multicultural Folktales: Stories to Tell Young Children*. Oryx, 1991, 136pp.

Caldecott Award Books

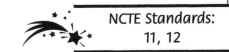

Caldecott Medal Winners

⭐ **Objective:**

Students will compare the illustrations in several Caldecott Medal winning books.

⭐ **Materials:**

★ Several Caldecott Medal Winner books

⭐ **Discussion:**

Hold up a Caldecott winner book and point to the gold seal on the cover.

Have you ever seen this gold medal on a book?

It's called the Caldecott Medal. It means this book won an award—a prize for the art.

An **illustrator** is the person who does the art for a book.

What supplies do artists use to create pictures?
(paints, watercolors, markers, pens, pencils, cut paper)

Why are the pictures in books important?

Do all books have pictures?

Why not?

The first Caldecott Award was given a long, long time ago—in 1938. Every year several books receive this award and one of those books is chosen as the best of them all.

Show students two Caldecott award books that have very different styles of artwork, like *Joseph Had a Little Overcoat* by Sims Taback and *Swimmy* by Leo Lionni.

Do not read the books at this time. Simply look at and talk about the illustrations.

How are the illustrations alike?

How are the illustrations different?

Which do you like better? Why?

What does the word illustrator mean?

What is the name of the award given to books with the best artwork?

Caldecott Award Books

Award Winners

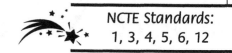

Objectives:

Students will design awards similar to the Caldecott Medal and select a book to receive the award.

Materials:

★ 10 or more Caldecott Medal award-winning books

★ Drawing paper and art materials

Discussion:

The Caldecott Medal is an award given each year to books with the best artwork.

These books (point to the Caldecott Medal winning books) all won the Caldecott Medal.

Books that won the Caldecott Medal have a gold medal on the front cover.

The first Caldecott Medal award was given in 1938.

What other types of awards or prizes do people win for being very good at something? (trophies, blue ribbons, etc.)

Activity: (part 1)

Students can use art supplies to design a different award for books with the best illustrations.

Tell students, the award can be a medal, like the Caldecott Award, or any other type of award.

Encourage students to use their imaginations and be creative.

Have each student include the name of the award either on the award itself or at the top of the page.

Activity: (part 2)

Give students time to look through the Caldecott Medal books available.

Ask each student to select the book with the artwork he or she likes best. If more than one student selects the same book, they can share it.

Display the awards they made and the books selected together for everyone to see.

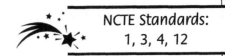

From a Picture to a Story

✴ Objective:

Students will create a story using only illustrations.

✴ Materials:

- ★ *Tuesday* by David Wiesner (several copies if possible)
- ★ Lined paper and pencils

✴ Preparation:

Make color copies of several pages from *Tuesday* unless you have lots of copies of the book.

✴ Discussion:

Can a story be told without pictures?

Can a story be told without words?

Can one picture tell a whole story?

✴ Activity:

Read *Tuesday* by David Wiesner.

For all or some of the illustrations, have students take turns "telling a story" about the picture. See variation described below for this section.

Remind students that stories should have a beginning, a middle, and an ending. Be sure students understand you want them to tell a story, not simply describe the picture.

Have students look through the book (and copies of the illustrations) individually and select one illustration for a story they will write. If possible, make extra copies of selected illustrations so each student will have one.

Students should write three or more sentences to tell a story about the illustration with a beginning, a middle, and an ending. Remind students to title their stories.

Very young children may need assistance with the actual writing, but make sure the sentences you help them write are theirs, not yours.

Ask students to take turns showing the appropriate illustration from the book and reading their stories to the group.

✴ Variation:

Have one student make up the beginning of a story about an illustration. A second student can continue the story and tell the middle part. A third student can finish the story by making up an ending.

Caldecott Award Books

A Story Without Words

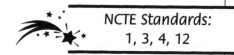

⭐ Objective:

Students will create a story using only illustrations.

⭐ Materials:

- ★ 4 sheets of art paper folded in half and stapled together at the fold to make a blank book for each student
- ★ Pencils, stapler
- ★ Art materials

⭐ Activity:

Give each student one blank book.

Tell students they will draw the parts of a story to make a book without words.

Read each part of the story on the next page slowly to the students. Repeat if necessary.

Stop after each part of the story. Give students time to draw a picture for that part of the story.

They should draw lightly with pencil, but not be overly concerned with details at this point.

Each part of the story should be drawn on a separate page in the book, starting on the second page.

Have students number the pages.

When the illustrations are finished, each student should write a title for the story and his or her name on the front cover.

Students can finish their pictures in class if time permits. If not, ask them to take their books home to finish.

Children can share their books with parents, relatives, and older siblings by showing the pictures and telling the story in their own words.

A Story Without Words (continued)

page 1   One day a child discovered an egg on the ground under a tree.

It was a small blue egg with white speckles.

"Why was the egg on the ground?" wondered the child.

The child looked closely. The egg did not seem to be broken.

page 2   The child looked up and saw a nest.

A mother bird was looking frantically around.

One of her eggs was missing!

Where could it be?

page 3   Then the mother bird saw her egg on the ground.

She saw the child looking at her egg.

What could she do?

The child seemed so big!

What if the child squashed her precious egg?

page 4   "I will scare the child away," thought the mother bird.

"Then I can save my egg."

She flew at the child and flapped her wings.

page 5   The child moved away from the egg and watched the mother bird.

The mother bird tried to lift her egg and put it back in the tree.

But it was too heavy.

page 6   Then the child came back.

Carefully, the child lifted the egg.

Gently, the child placed the egg back in the nest.

page 7   Then the child waved to the mother bird and went home.

Caldecott Award Books

Alike and Different

⭐ Objectives:

Students will verbally compare and contrast two objects and will learn how to complete a Venn diagram.

⭐ Materials:

- ★ An orange and an apple
- ★ Classroom pet or stuffed animal

⭐ Discussion:

Draw a large Venn diagram on the board. Label one side "apple" and one side "orange." Label the section where the circles intersect: "apples and oranges."

Hold up an apple and an orange.

As students answer the questions, write their responses in the appropriate parts of the Venn diagram. Let student volunteers point to where the information belongs.

How are an apple and an orange alike?

(Both are fruits; both are round; both can be eaten; both have seeds; both can be peeled; both are healthy, etc.)

How are an apple and an orange different?

(Taste, color, size, etc.)

What can you do with an orange, that you can't do with an apple? (Make orange juice, peel it with your fingers, etc.)

What can you do with an apple, that you can't do with an orange? (Make a pie, make applesauce, make apple juice, jelly, or cider, etc.)

Repeat the comparison and contrast questions for the apple and your classroom pet. If you do not have any live animals, even fish, use a stuffed animal, but ask students to pretend it is real.

Complete another Venn diagram for these the apple and the animal. This time students will probably find more differences than similarities.

Besides an apple and an orange, what else could we compare using a Venn diagram?

Could we compare the characters, plots, settings, or themes in two books using a Venn diagram?

Comparison and Contrast

⭐ Objective:

Students will compare and contrast two Caldecott books.

⭐ Materials:

- ★ *Anansi the Spider* by Gerald McDermott
- ★ *A Story! A Story!* by Gail Haley.
- ★ Other book pairs (See Caldecott bibliography for suggested pairs)
- ★ Pencils and paper

⭐ Discussion:

We can look for ways two pieces of fruit are alike and different.

We can also look for ways two stories are alike and different.

Read *Anansi the Spider* by Gerald McDermott and *A Story! A Story!* by Gail Haley. Then continue with the discussion questions.

How were the main characters in the two books alike?

How were they different?

How were the settings alike?

How were they different?

How were the plots alike?

How were they different?

How were the themes alike?

How were they different?

How were the illustrations alike?

How were they different?

⭐ Activity:

Have students work with a partner. Give each pair two books. Have students read both books, then complete a Venn diagram together comparing only one aspect of the books: main characters, plots, settings, or themes.

If students are prereaders, complete the activity for another pair of books as a group.

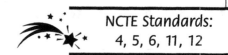

NCTE Standards:
4, 5, 6, 11, 12

Tops and Bottoms: A Puppet Show

⭐ Objectives:

Students will communicate with an audience by presenting a puppet show based on the book *Tops and Bottoms*. They will use fluency and expression in oral reading.

⭐ Materials:

- ★ *Tops and Bottoms* by Janet Stevens
- ★ One copy of the script, "Tops and Bottoms" for each student who will be reading a part
- ★ Yellow marker
- ★ Paint stir sticks
- ★ Reproducibles of the characters for the play
- ★ Masking tape
- ★ Stapler
- ★ Scissors

⭐ Preparation:

1. Prepare each copy of the script by highlighting all the speaking parts for one of the characters, i.e., one copy highlighting the narrator's words, one highlighting Mr. Hare's words, etc.

2. Staple pages for each set together.

⭐ Discussion:

Many movies are based on books that someone wrote like *Charlotte's Web* by E. B. White and *How the Grinch Stole Christmas* by Dr. Seuss.

What other movies have you seen that were based on books you've read or heard?

Which did you like better, the book or the movie? Why?

⭐ Activity:

Read *Tops and Bottoms* to the group.

Tell students they will be presenting a puppet show about this book.

Tops and Bottoms: A Puppet Show *(continued)*

Assign several students to be the "puppet masters" and other students to read the parts of various characters in the script.

Depending on the number of students in the group, the narrator's parts can be read by five different students or combined and read by only one or two.

All students should participate in the puppet show in the same manner.

Have students work together to cut out and color the characters for the play.

Tape the back of each character to a paint stir stick.

The puppet masters will sit behind a desk and raise the puppets at the appropriate times in the script.

Give students their highlighted copies of the script.

Read through the script, cuing students when it is their turn to read their parts.

Practice the script as a group until students can read their parts fluently and with expression and puppet masters know when to hold up each character.

Give students extra individual attention if needed.

Encourage students to practice reading their parts at home with parents or older siblings.

Students can present the play to other classes, at a school assembly, or as part of a family night gathering.

Tops and Bottoms

An African-American folk tale retold by Janet Stevens
Scripted by Annie Weissman

Characters: *Narrator(s), Bear, Mr. Hare, Mrs. Hare, Hare's Children*

Narrator 1: Once upon a time there lived a very lazy bear who had lots of money and lots of land. His father had been a hard worker and a smart business bear. He had given all his money and land to his son.

Bear: All I want to do is sleep.

Narrator 2: Not far down the road lived a family of hares. Although Mr. Hare was clever, he sometimes got into trouble.

Mr. Hare: I once owned land, too. But now I have nothing. I lost a risky bet with a tortoise and sold all of my land to Bear to pay off the debt.

Mrs. Hare: We are in very bad shape.

Hare's children: We are so hungry!

Mrs. Hare: We must think of something!

Narrator 3: So Mr. and Mrs. Hare put their heads together and cooked up a plan. The next day Mr. Hare hopped down the road to Bear's house. As usual, Bear was asleep.

Mr. Hare: Hello, Bear! Wake up! It's your neighbor, Mr. Hare. I have an idea.

Bear: Grunt, grunt!

Mr. Hare: We can be business partners. All we need is this field right here in front of your house. I'll do the hard work of planting and harvesting. We can split the profits right down the middle. Yes, sir, Bear. We're in this together. I'll work and you'll sleep.

Bear: Huh?

Mr. Hare: So what will it be Bear? The top half or the bottom half? It's up to you—tops or bottoms?

Bear: Uh, let's see. I'll take the top half, Mr. Hare. Right, tops.

Mr. Hare: It's a done deal.

Narrator 4: So Bear went back to sleep and Mr. Hare and his family went to work.

Mr. Hare: I'm planting!

Mrs. Hare: I'm watering!

Mr. Hare's children: We're weeding!

Narrator 5: Bear slept as the crops grew. Finally it was time for the harvest.

Mr. Hare: Wake up, Bear! You get the tops and I get the bottoms.

Narrator 1: Mr. Hare and his family dug up the carrots, the radishes, and the beets.

Mr. Hare: I'm plucking off the tops and tossing them into a pile for Bear. I'll keep the bottoms: all the carrots, radishes and beets, for my family!

Bear: I'm looking at my pile, Mr. Hare. How come you have all the best parts in your half?

Mr. Hare: You chose the tops, Bear.

Bear: Mr. Hare, you tricked me! You plant this field again. This season I want the bottoms!

Mr. Hare: It's a done deal, Bear.

Narrator 2: So Bear went back to sleep. Mr. Hare and his family went back to work.

Mr. Hare: I'm planting!

Mrs. Hare: I'm watering!

Hare's children: We're weeding!

Narrator 3: Bear slept as the crops grew.

Mr. Hare: It's time for the harvest. Wake up, Bear! You get the bottoms and I get the tops.

Mrs. Hare: Our family is gathering the lettuce, the broccoli, and the celery.

Hare's children: We're pulling off the bottoms for Bear and putting the tops in our family's pile.

Bear: I'm looking at my pile and I am not happy! Mr. Hare, you tricked me again.

Mr. Hare: But Bear, you wanted the bottoms this time.

Bear: Growl! You plant this field again, Mr. Hare. You've tricked me twice and you owe me one season of both tops and bottoms!

Mr. Hare: You're right, poor old Bear. It's only fair that you get both tops and bottoms this time. It's a done deal, Bear.

Narrator 4: So Bear went back to sleep.

Mr. Hare: I'm planting!

Mrs. Hare: I'm watering!

Hare's children: We're weeding!

Narrator 5: Bear slept as the crops grew.

Mr. Hare: It's time for the harvest. Wake up, Bear! This time you get the tops and the bottoms.

Narrator 1: Bear looked out and saw a field of tall corn.

Mrs. Hare: Let's yank up every cornstalk.

Mr. Hare: I'll tug off the roots at the bottoms and the tassels at the top and put them in a pile for Bear.

Hare's children: We'll collect the ears of corn in the middle and place them in our family's pile.

Mr. Hare: See, Bear. You get the tops and the bottoms. I get the middles. Yes, sir, Bear. It's a done deal!

Bear: That's it, Mr. Hare! From now on I'll plant my own crops and take the tops, bottoms, and the middles! I'm not going to sleep through a season of planting and harvesting again!

Narrator 2: Mr. Hare and his family scooped up the corn. They hopped down the road toward home.

Mr. Hare: We can buy back our land with the profit from the crops.

Mrs. Hare: I'm going to open a vegetable stand.

Narrator 3: Mr. Hare and Bear learned to live happily as neighbors, but they were never business partners again.

Bear Puppet

Mr. Hare Puppet

Mrs. Hare Puppet

Children Hares

Caldecott Book Pairs

These pairs of Caldecott books work well for comparison and contrast activities.

Blueberries for Sal by Robert McCloskey and *The Biggest Bear* by Lynd Ward

Hush! A Thai Lullaby by Minfong Ho and *Ten, Nine, Eight* by Molly Bang

It Could Always Be Worse by Margot Zemach and *Frederick* by Leo Lionni

Joseph Had a Little Overcoat by Simms Taback and *Seven Blind Mice* by Ed Young

May I Bring a Friend? by Beatrice Schenk de Regniers and *McElligot's Pool* by Dr. Seuss

Mufaro's Beautiful Daughters by John Steptoe and *Cinderella* by Marcia Brown

No, David! by David Shannon and *Yo! Yes!* by Chris Raschka

Snow by Uri Shulevitz and *The Snowy Day* by Ezra Jack Keats

The Big Snow by Berta and Elmer Hader and *Snowflake Bentley* by Jacqueline Briggs Martin

The Funny Little Woman by Arlene Mosel and *Where the Wild Things Are* by Maurice Sendak

Tuesday by David Wiesner and *Frog Went A' Courtin'* by John Langstaff

Caldecott Books Arranged by Literary Elements

Character

Ackerman, Karen, *Song and Dance Man*. Knopf, 1988.

Bang, Molly, *When Sophie Gets Angry— Really, Really Angry*. Scholastic, 1999.

Goble, Paul, *The Girl Who Loved Wild Horses*. Simon & Schuster, 1983.

Henkes, Kevin, *Owen*. Greenwillow, 1993.

Lionni, Leo, *Alexander and the Wind-Up Mouse*. Knopf, 1969.

Lobel, Arnold, *Frog and Toad Are Friends*. HarperCollins, 1970.

McCully, Emily Arnold, *Mirette on the High Wire*. Putnam, 1992.

Ringold, Faith, *Tar Beach*. Crown, 1991.

Williams, Vera B., *A Chair for My Mother*. Greenwillow, 1983.

Setting

Bang, Molly, *Ten, Nine, Eight*. Greenwillow, 1983.

Bunting, Eve, *Smoky Night*. Harcourt, 1994.

Burton, Virginia Lee, *The Little House*. Houghton, 1969.

Feelings, Muriel, *Moja Means One*. Dial, 1971.

Isadora, Rachel, *Ben's Trumpet*. Greenwillow, 1979.

McCloskey, Robert, *Make Way for Ducklings*. Viking, 1969.

Shulevitz, Uri, *Snow*. Farrar, 1998.

Van Allsburg, Chris, *The Polar Express*. Houghton, 1985.

Wood, Audrey, *King Bidgood's in the Bathtub*. Harcourt, 1985.

Yolen, Jane, *Owl Moon*. Philomel, 1987.

Caldecott Books Arranged by Literary Elements *(continued)*

Plot

DePaola, Tomie, *Strega Nona*. Prentice Hall, 1975.

Haley, Gail E., *A Story! A Story!* Atheneum, 1970.

Keats, Ezra Jack, *Goggles*. Viking, 1998.

Kimmel, Eric A., *Hershel and the Hanukkah Goblins*. Holiday House, 1989.

Lester, Julius, *John Henry*. Dial, 1994.

Mosel, Arlene, *The Funny Little Woman*. Dutton, 1972.

Sendak, Maurice, *Where the Wild Things Are*. HarperCollins, 1984.

Shannon, David, *No, David!* Scholastic, 1998.

Snyder, Dianne, *The Boy of the Three Year Nap*. Houghton, 1988.

Steig, William, *Dr. De Soto*. Scholastic, 1982.

Steig, William, *Sylvester and the Magic Pebble*. Simon & Schuster, 1969.

Wisniewski, David, *Golem*. Clarion, 1996.

Young, Ed, *Lon Po Po: A Red-Riding Hood Story from China*. Philomel, 1989.

Zelinsky, Paul O., *Rapunzel*. Dutton, 1997.

Point of view

Birnbaum, A., *Green Eyes*. Capitol, 1953.

Lobel, Arnold, *On Market Street*. Greenwillow, 1981.

Raschka, Chris, *Yo! Yes!* Orchard, 1993.

Rylant, Cynthia, *When I Was Young in the Mountains*. Dutton, 1982.

Stewart, Sarah, *The Gardener*. Farrar, 1997.

Theme

Andersen, Hans Christian, *Ugly Duckling* (illustrated by Jerry Pinkney). Morrow, 1999.

Brown, Marcia, *Once a Mouse . . . .* Scribner, 1961.

Cooney, Barbara, *Chanticleer and the Fox*. Crowell, 1958.

Lionni, Leo, *Frederick*. Knopf, 1987.

Lionni, Leo, *Swimmy*. Pantheon, 1963.

Lipkind, William, and Nicolas, Mordvinoff *Finders Keepers*. Harcourt, 1989.

Lobel, Arnold, *Fables*. HarperCollins, 1980.

Rathmann, Peggy, *Officer Buckle and Gloria*. Putnam, 1995

Shulevitz, Uri, *The Treasure*. Farrar, 1979.

Yorinks, Arthur, *Hey, Al*. Farrar, 1986.

Young, Ed, *Seven Blind Mice*. Philomel, 1992.

Zemach, Harve, *The Judge: An Untrue Tale*. Farrar, 1969.

Zemach, Margot, *It Could Always Be Worse*. Farrar, 1990.

Folk Tales

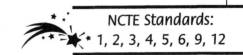

Elements of Folk Tales

=★ **Objective:**

Students will apply what they learned about the elements of fiction to folk tales.

=★ **Materials:**

- ★ *Why Mosquitoes Buzz in People's Ears* by Berna Aardema
- ★ *One Fine Day* by Nonny Hogrogian
- ★ *Mice Twice* by Joseph Low
- ★ One copy of "Tell Me About a Folk Tale" for each student
- ★ Pencils

=★ **Discussion:**

Folk tales are stories about people and places that aren't real.

Like all stories, folk tales have main characters.

The main characters of folk tales can be people, animals, or nonliving things, like the sun or the north wind.

The setting for folk tales is usually the past. Many folk tales begin with the words, "Long, long ago . . ." or "Once Upon a time . . ."

What stories do you know that begin with those words?

The plot of a story includes the events that happen, in order.

=★ **Activity:**

Read one of the books listed to the group.

Ask these questions.

Who is the main character?

Where does the story take place?

When does the story take place?

What happens in the story?

What is the problem?

How is it solved?

What is the theme of the story?

From whose point of view is the story told?

Read another folk tale to the group.

Give each student a copy of "Tell Me About a Folk Tale." Students can complete this activity as a group, with a partner, or individually.

This reproducible can also be used for other folk tales.

Tell Me About a Folk Tale

Who is the main character?

_____

List three main events.

1. _____

_____

2. _____

_____

3. _____

_____

When did the story take place?

_____

_____

Where did the story take place?

_____

_____

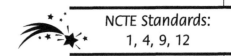

The Castle of Chuchurumbel

⭐ Objectives:

Students will listen to and will join in telling a repetitive folk tale and will then illustrate the tale sequentially.

⭐ Materials:

- ★ The "Castle of Chuchurumbel" script
- ★ One copy of the "Castle of Chuchurumbel" reproducible for each student
- ★ Colored pencils and crayons

⭐ Activity:

Read "The Castle of Chuchurumbel" to the group.

Encourage students to join in on repetitive phrases.

Give each student a copy of the "Castle of Chuchurumbel" reproducible.

Read the story again. This time, pause after reading each section while students draw in the details.

Read "These are the doors of the Castle of Chuchurumbel." Pause while students draw the door.

Read "These are the keys that opened the doors of the Castle of Chuchurumbel." Pause while students draw the keys.

Continue until the end of the story.

When all the elements are added, students can color the pictures.

Display student work on the bulletin board.

Encourage students to take their illustrations home and retell the story to friends and family members.

Name ____________________ Date ____________________

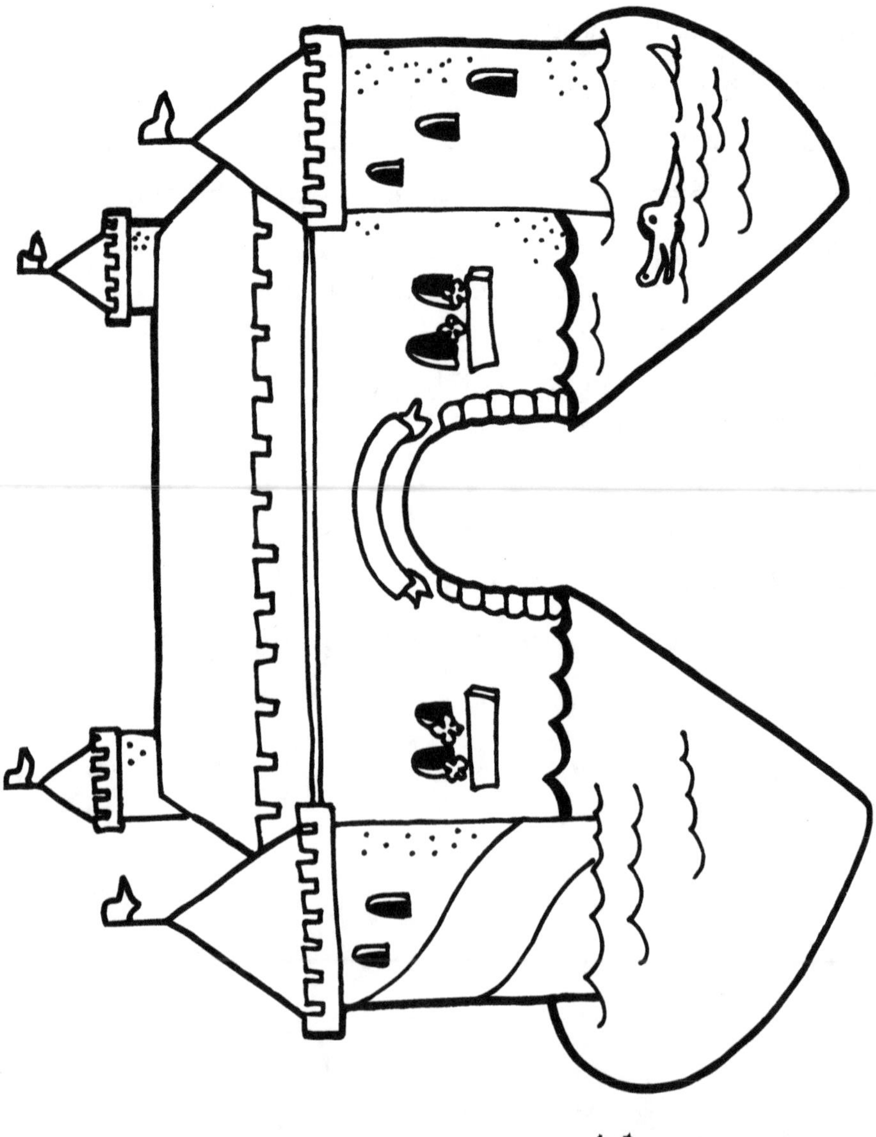

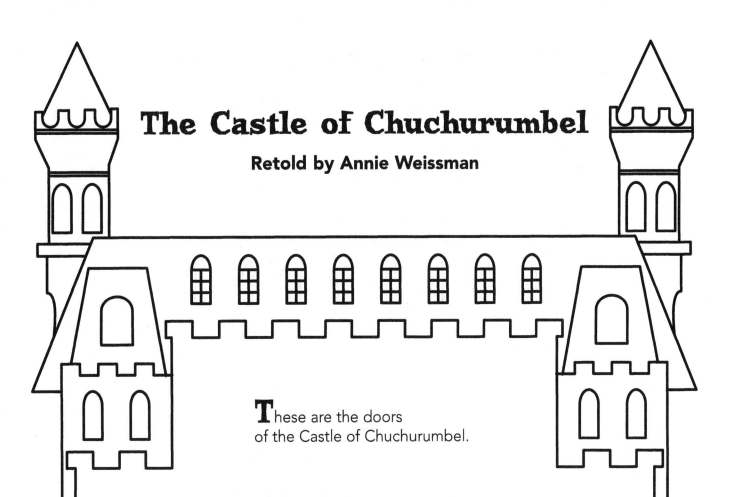

The Castle of Chuchurumbel

Retold by Annie Weissman

These are the doors
of the Castle of Chuchurumbel.

These are the keys
that opened the doors
of the Castle of Chuchurumbel.

This is the cord
that held the keys
that opened the doors
of the Castle of Chuchurumbel.

This is the rat
that chewed the cord
that held the keys
that opened the doors
of the Castle of Chuchurumbel.

This is the cat
that ate the rat
that chewed the cord
that held the keys
that opened the doors
of the Castle of Chuchurumbel.

This is the dog
that chased the cat
that ate the rat
that chewed the cord
that held the keys
that opened the doors
of the Castle of Chuchurumbel.

This is the stick
that hit the dog
that chased the cat
that ate the rat
that chewed the cord
that held the keys
that opened the doors
of the Castle of Chuchurumbel.

The Castle of Chuchurumbel (continued)

This is the fire
that burned the stick
that hit the dog
that chased the cat
that ate the rat
that chewed the cord
that held the keys
that opened the doors
of the Castle of Chuchurumbel.

This is the water
that put out the fire
that burned the stick
that hit the dog
that chased the cat
that ate the rat
that chewed the cord
that held the keys
that opened the doors
of the Castle of Chuchurumbel.

This is the ox
that drank the water
that put out the fire
that burned the stick
that hit the dog
that chased the cat
that ate the rat
that chewed the cord
that held the keys
that opened the doors
of the Castle of Chuchurumbel.

These are the people
of the Castle of Chuchurumbel
who own the ox
that drank the water
that put out the fire
that burned the stick
that hit the dog
that chased the cat
that ate the rat
that chewed the cord
that held the keys
that opened the doors
of the Castle of Chuchurumbel.

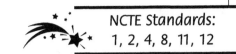

Around the World with Folk Tales

⭐ Objectives:

Students will listen to folk tales from other countries and locate the countries on a world map or globe. Students will compare the setting of the story to our present day environment.

⭐ Materials:

- ★ A large world map or globe
- ★ *Stone Soup* by Marcia Brown

⭐ Activity:

This globe (map) shows all the countries.

Let's find where we live.

We live on the continent of North America. (point)

In the country called the United States. (point)

In the state of . . . (point)

And our city, . . ., is right about there. (point)

Many stories we read were first told in other countries. Some of the countries are far away.

Have you ever seen the movie or heard the story about "Beauty and the Beast?"

That story was first told in France.

Keep a finger of one hand on the place where you live and use the other hand to point out France on the map or globe.

"Cinderella" is another story from France.

"Little Red Riding Hood" and "Rapunzel" are stories from Germany.

Let's find Germany together. It's near France.

"Anansi the Spider" came from a country in Africa called Ghana.

Find Africa together, then point to Ghana.

"Jack and the Beanstalk" came from England.

Today we're going to read a story from France.

Read *Stone Soup* to the group.

Around the World with Folk Tales *(continued)*

Draw a large Venn diagram on the board. Write "Stone Soup" above the left circle and "present day" above the right circle.

As students answer the discussion questions, write the similarities and differences in the appropriate parts of the Venn diagram.

⚡ Discussion:

The setting of a story is where and when it takes place.

When do you think *Stone Soup* took place: past, present, or future?

What clues from the story tell us it took place in the past? (illustrations and text)

Where does the story take place?

How is the clothing worn by the characters like clothing we wear?

How is it different?

How are the people like us?

How are they different?

How is the food mentioned like food we eat?

How is it different?

How is the place where the people live different?

How is it like where people in the United States live?

What other way is the setting of the story different?

Read two other folk tales. See the bibliography at the end of this section for suggestions.

Have students complete a Venn diagram to compare and contrast the settings and characters of the two stories. This can be done as a group or individually.

⚡ Future Activities:

Before reading other folk tales from different countries, help students find the country on the globe or map.

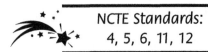

Directing and Planning a Presentation

Objective:

Students will create and follow a plan for a group presentation of "I Know an Old Lady Who Swallowed a Fly" to an audience.

Materials:

★ Several different illustrated versions of "I Know an Old Lady Who Swallowed a Fly" (One that children seem to particularly enjoy is the die-cut version, *There Was An Old Woman* by Simms Taback.)

★ One copy of the script for "I Know an Old Woman Who Swallowed a Fly" for each student who will be reading a part

★ Yellow marker and stapler

★ Art and craft supplies

Preparation:

1. Prepare each copy of the play by highlighting all the speaking parts for each student, i.e., on one copy, highlight only the words for student 1, on another, highlight only the words for student 2, etc.

2. Staple pages for each set together.

Activity:

Read your favorite illustrated version of "I Know an Old Lady Who Swallowed a Fly."

Sometimes more than one author or artist decides to write a book about the same basic story.

Show students other books that present this same story/song and let them look for similarities and differences.

Discussion:

We are going to do a presentation of "I Know an Old Woman Who Swallowed a Fly."

I have scripts we can use for reading.

The rest is up to you to decide how to do this story in our own special way.

Directing and Planning a Presentation *(continued)*

For example, we could do this as a puppet show and make our own puppets for the old woman and each animal she swallowed.

What other ways could we present this story?

(Encourage students to contribute ideas. Write one or two words on the board for each idea, i.e., puppet show, play, song and dance, etc.)

Let students vote on their favorite suggestion. If they decided on a puppet show, they will need to decide what kind of puppets to make and how to make them.

⭐ Activity:

Once they have decided on a way to present the material, help students work out the details. Students can work in groups on different aspects of the presentation, artwork, props, invitations, etc.

At the appropriate time, assign students reading parts for the script and give them their copies.

For the chorus, all students speak together.

Read through the script with them. Cue students when it is their turn to read specific parts. Cue the group when it is time for all to speak together.

Encourage students to practice reading their parts at home with parents or older siblings.

Practice the play as a group until students are comfortable with their parts. This can be done each day shortly before or after working on the other parts of the presentation.

Students can perform their presentation for other classes in the library, at a school assembly, or as part of a Family Night gathering.

I Know an Old Lady Who Swallowed a Fly

An Old English folksong

1 I know an old lady who swallowed a fly.

ALL I don't know why she swallowed a fly,
Perhaps she'll die.

2 I know an old lady who swallowed a spider.
It wriggled and jiggled and tickled inside her.
She swallowed the spider to catch the fly.

ALL I don't know why she swallowed a fly,
Perhaps she'll die.

3 I know an old lady who swallowed a bird.
How absurd! She swallowed a bird!
She swallowed the bird to catch the spider,
That wriggled and jiggled and tickled inside her.

2 She swallowed the spider to catch the fly.

ALL I don't know why she swallowed a fly,
Perhaps she'll die.

4 I know an old lady who swallowed a cat.
Imagine that! She swallowed a cat!
She swallowed the cat to catch the bird.

3 She swallowed the bird to catch the spider,
That wriggled and jiggled and tickled inside her.

2 She swallowed the spider to catch the fly.

ALL I don't know why she swallowed a fly,
Perhaps she'll die.

5 I know an old lady who swallowed a dog.
My what a hog! She swallowed a dog!
She swallowed the dog to catch the cat.

4   She swallowed the cat to catch the bird.

3   She swallowed the bird to catch the spider,
That wriggled and jiggled and tickled inside her.

2   She swallowed the spider to catch the fly.

ALL I don't know why she swallowed a fly,
Perhaps she'll die.

6   I know an old lady who swallowed a goat.
Just opened her throat and swallowed that goat!
She swallowed the goat to catch the dog.

5   She swallowed the dog to catch the cat.

4   She swallowed the cat to catch the bird.

3   She swallowed the bird to catch the spider,
That wriggled and jiggled and tickled inside her.

2   She swallowed the spider to catch the fly.

ALL I don't know why she swallowed a fly,
Perhaps she'll die.

7   I know an old lady who swallowed a cow.
I don't know how she swallowed a cow!
She swallowed the cow to catch the goat.

6   She swallowed the goat to catch the dog.

5   She swallowed the dog to catch the cat.

4   She swallowed the cat to catch the bird.

3   She swallowed the bird to catch the spider,
That wriggled and jiggled and tickled
inside her.

2   She swallowed the spider to catch the fly.

ALL I don't know why she swallowed a fly,
Perhaps she'll die.

8   I know an old lady who swallowed a horse.

ALL She's dead, of course!

Tales That Emphasize Comparison and Contrast

Fools and Tricksters

Birdseye, Tom, *Soap! Soap! Don't Forget the Soap!* Holiday House, 1993.

DePaola, Tomie, *Fin M'Coul.* Holiday House, 1981.

Goble, Paul, *Iktomi and the Buffalo Skull.* Orchard, 1991.

Hamilton, Virginia, *A Ring of Tricksters.* Blue Sky Press, 1997.

LaCapa, Michael, *The Flute Player.* Northland, 1990.

Walker, Barbara, *Just Say Hic.* Follett, 1965.

Wardlaw, Lee, *Punia and the King of the Sharks.* Dial, 1997.

Williams, Jay, *The Wicked Tricks of Tyl Uilenspiegel.* Four Winds, 1975.

Pourquoi tales

Aardema, Verna, *Why Mosquitoes Buzz In People's Ears.* Dial, 1975.

Bruchac, Joseph, and Ross, Gayle, *The Story of the Milky Way.* Dial, 1995.

Duncan, Lois, *The Magic of the Spider Woman.* Scholastic, 1996.

Heroes and Heroines

DePaola, Tomie, *The Legend of the Indian Paintbrush.* Putnam, 1988.

Kurtz, Jane, *Miro in the Kingdom of the Sun.* Houghton Mifflin, 1996.

Sabuda, Robert, *Arthur and the Sword.* Atheneum, 1995.

San Souci, Robert D., *Brave Margaret.* Simon & Schuster, 1999.

San Souci, Robert D., *Young Arthur.* Doubleday, 1997.

Bibliography of Tales by Country

England

DeLaMare, Walter, *Molly Whuppie.* Farrar, 1983.

Galdone, Paul, *King of Cats.* Houghton, 1980.

Hodges, Margaret, *Molly Limbo.* Atheneum, 1996.

Huck, Charlotte, *Princess Furball.* Greenwillow, 1989.

Kellogg, Steven, *The Three Sillies.* Candlewick, 1999.

Kimmel, Eric A., *The Old Woman and Her Pig.* Holiday House, 1992.

Robins, Arthur, *The Teeny Tiny Woman.* Candlewick, 1998.

Ross, Tony, *Lazy Jack.* Dial, 1986.

Sabuda, Robert, *Arthur and the Sword.* Atheneum, 1995.

Shulevitz, Uri, *The Treasure.* Farrar, 1978.

Taback, Simms, *There Was an Old Woman.* Viking, 1997.

Wells, Rosemary, *Jack and the Beanstalk.* DK, 1997.

Williams, Marcia, *King Arthur and the Knights of the Round Table.* Candlewick, 1996.

Zemach, Harve, *Duffy and the Devil.* Farrar, 1973.

Bibliography of Tales by Country (continued)

France

Bauman, Kurt, *Puss in Boots*. North-South, 1999.

Brett, Jan, *Beauty and the Beast*. Clarion, 1989.

Brown, Marcia, *Stone Soup*. Aladdin, 1997, 1947.

DeFelice, Cynthia C., *Three Perfect Peaches*. Orchard, 1995.

Ehrlich, Amy, *Cinderella*. Dial, 1985.

Huck, Charlotte S., *Toads and Diamonds*. Greenwillow, 1995.

Perrault, Charles, *Cinderella and Other Tales from Perrault*. Holt, 1989.

Germany

Geringer, Laura, *The Seven Ravens*. HarperCollins, 1994.

Hyman, Trina Schart, *Little Red Riding Hood*. Holiday House, 1998, 1983.

Kimmel, Eric A., *Seven at One Blow: A Tale from the Brothers Grimm*. Holiday House, 1998.

Lesser, Riuka, *Hansel and Gretel*. Dutton, 1999.

Lippert, Meg, *Finest the Falcon*. Troll, 1996.

McDermott, Dennis, *The Golden Goose*. Morrow, 2000.

Ormerod, Jan, *The Frog Prince*. Lothrop, 1990.

Ray, Jane, *The Twelve Dancing Princesses*. Dutton, 1999.

Stevens, Janet, *The Bremen Town Musicians*. Holiday House, 1992.

Zelinsky, Paul O., *Rapunzel*. Dutton, 1997.

Zelinsky, Paul O., *Rumpelstilskin*. Dutton, 1986.

Russia

Cole, Joanna, *Bony-Legs*. Four Winds, 1986.

Davis, Aubrey, *The Enormous Potato*. Kids Can, 1998.

Ginsburg, Mirra, *Clay Boy*. Greenwillow, 1997.

Kimmel, Eric A., *I-Know-Not-What, I-Know-Not-Where*. Holiday House, 1994.

Lurie, Alison, *The Black Geese: A Baba Yaga Tale from Russia*. DK, 1999.

McCaughrean, Geraldine, *Grandma Chickenlegs*. Carolrhoda, 1999.

Peck, Jan, *The Giant Carrot*. Dial, 1998.

Rafe, Martin, *The Language of Birds*. Putnam, 2000.

Ransome, Arthur, *The Fool of the World and the Flying Ship*. Farrar, 1987.

San Souci, Robert D., *Peter and the Blue Witch Baby*. Doubleday, 2000.

Ziefert, Harriet, *The Snow Child*. Puffin, 2000.

Japan

Compton, Patricia A., *The Terrible Eek*. Simon & Schuster, 1991.

Hamanaka, Sheila, *Screen of Frogs*. Orchard, 1993.

Minarik, Rosemary, "Three Strong Women" from *Womenfolk and Fairy Tales*. Houghton Mifflin, 1975.

Mosel, Arlene, *The Funny Little Woman*. Dutton, 1972.

San Souci, Robert D., *The Samurai's Daughter*. Puffin, 1997.

Snyder, Dianne, *The Boy of the Three Year Nap*. Houghton, 1988.

Bibliography of Tales by Country (continued)

China

Chang, Margaret, *Scrojin, Da Wei's Treasure*. Margaret K. Elderberry, 1999.

Demi, *Liang and the Magic Paintbrush*. Holt, 1980.

Mosel, Arlene. *Tikki Tikki Tembo*. Dutton, 1968.

San Souci, Robert D., *Fa Mulan*. Hyperion, 1998.

Yep, Laurence, *The Boy Who Swallowed Snakes*. Scholastic, 1994.

Young, Ed, *Lon Po Po: A Red-Riding Hood Story from China*. Philomel, 1989.

Young, Ed, *The Terrible Nung Gwama*. Collins & World, 1976.

India

Brown, Marcia, *Once a Mouse . . .* Scribner, 1961.

Demi, *A Grain of Rice*. Scholastic, 1997.

Duff, Maggie, *Rum Pum Pum*. Macmillan, 1978.

Galdone, Paul, *The Monkey and the Crocodile*. Seabury, 1969.

Iran

Cohen, Barbara, *Seven Daughters & Seven Sons*. Atheneum, 1982.

Kherdian, David, *The Smile of the Rose*. Holt, 1997.

Kimmel, Eric A., *Ali Baba and the Forty Thieves*. Holiday House, 1996.

Turkey

Sierra, Judy, "Eat, Coat, Eat!" from *Multicultural Folktales for the Feltboard and Readers' Theater*. Oryx, 1996.

Walker, Barbara, *Just Say Hic*. Follett, 1965.

Israel

(Jewish folktales, not necessarily set in Israel)

Freedman, Florence B., *Brothers*. Harper & Row, 1985.

Gilman, Phoebe, *Something from Nothing*. Scholastic, 1992.

Hirsch, Marilyn, *The Rabbi and the Twenty-Nine Witches*. Holiday House, 1976.

Kimmel, Eric A., *Onions and Garlic*. Holiday House, 1996.

Wisniewski, David, *The Golem*. Clarion, 1996.

Zemach, Margot, *It Could Always Be Worse*. Farrar, 1990.

Ghana

Chocolate, Deborah M., *Talk! Talk!* Troll, 1993.

Kimmel, Eric A., *Anansi and the Moss-Covered Rock*. Holiday House, 1988.

Lake, Mary, *The Royal Drum*. Mondo, 1996.

McDermott, Gerald, *Anansi the Spider*. Holt, 1972.

Mollel, Tololwa M., *Ananse's Feast*. Clarion, 1997.

Bibliography of Tales by Country (continued)

Mexico

Aardema, Verna, *Borreguita and the Coyote*. Random, 1981.

Ada, Alma Flor, *The Lizard in the Sun/La lagartija y el sol*. Doubleday, 1997.

Ehlert, Lois, *Cuckoo: A Mexican Tale/Cucu: un cuento folklorico mexicana*. Harcourt Brace, 1997.

Johnston, Tony, *The Tale of Rabbit and Coyote*. Putnam, 1994.

Lyons, Grant, "The Marvelous Chirionerra" from *Tales the People Tell in Mexico*. Messner, 1972.

Sauvageau, Juan, "The Ungrateful Snake" from *Tales That Must Not Die Volume I*. Oasis, 1984.

Weissman, Annie, *The Castle of Chuchurumbel/El castillo de Chuchurumbel*. Hispanic Books Distributors, 1987.

United States

Chase, Richard, "*Soap! Soap! Soap!*" from *The Grandfather Tales*. Houghton Mifflin, 1948.

Courlander, Harold, "The Beetle's Hairpiece" from *People of the Short Blue Corn*. Harcourt, 1970.

Davis, Aubrey, *Sody Sallyratus*. Kids Can, 1998.

Hayes, Joe, *The Day It Snowed Tortillas*. Mariposa, 1985.

Hayes, Joe, *Soft Child: How Rattlesnake Got Its Fangs*. Roberts Rhinehart, 1993.

Lester, Julius, "Why Dogs Hate Cats" from *The Knee-High Man and Other Tales*. Dial, 1972.

Sloat, Terri, *Sody Sallyratus*. Dutton, 1997.

Fantasy

That's Fantastic!

⭐ Objective:

Students will distinguish between fantasy and events that are real.

⭐ Materials:

★ One copy of "Real or Fantasy?" for each student

★ Crayons

⭐ Discussion:

What does fantasy mean? (Elicit a response that indicates students understand that fantasy means not real.)

Sometimes the characters in a fantasy are animals that talk and act like people.

What cartoon animals talk and act like people?

The characters in a fantasy may be people who can do things that real people can't do, like fly or become invisible.

What can Spiderman do that real people can't do?

Who is another cartoon character with special abilities?

Fantasy stories often take place somewhere that isn't real.

Is the place where Ash and Pikachu live a real place?

Things can happen in a fantasy that don't happen in real life.

Houses could be make of candy; popcorn snow could fall from the sky.

Activity:

Give each student a copy of the "Real or Fantasy?" page to complete.

When they finish, talk about why the pictures they colored could not be real.

Name _____   Date _____

Real or Fantasy?

Color the pictures that are fantasy.

Fantasy

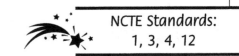

Is Dear Duck a Real Duck?

⭐ Objective:

Students will compare the main character in *Happy Birthday, Dear Duck* to real ducks

⭐ Materials:

- ★ *Happy Birthday, Dear Duck* by Eve Bunting
- ★ *Ducking Days* by Karen Wallace
- ★ One copy of "Real Ducks and Dear Duck" for each student
- ★ Pencils and crayons
- ★ Art paper

⭐ Discussion:

What can Mickey Mouse do that mice can't do in real life?

Do real mice wear clothes?

Can real mice ride bicycles or drive cars?

How else is Mickey Mouse different than a real mouse?

⭐ Activity:

Read *Duckling Days* to the group.

Ask students to list "facts" they learned about ducks.

Read *Happy Birthday, Dear Duck* to the group.

What does Dear Duck do that real ducks can do?

What does Dear Duck do that real ducks can't do?

Give each student a copy of "Real Ducks and Dear Duck."

Complete the activity together.

Have students draw fantasy characters for their own stories. Ask students to show their drawings to the group and tell a short story about the character.

Display students' drawings of fantasy characters for them to use for ideas when they complete the activity, "Characters, Setting, and Plot."

⭐ Reinforcement:

Read other pairs of nonfiction and fantasy books about animals for students to compare. A list of suggestions for pairing is included in the bibliography at the end of this section.

Name _____ Date _____

Real Ducks and Dear Duck

How real ducks look: _____

_____

What real ducks do: _____

_____

How Dear Duck looks: _____

_____

What Dear Duck does: _____

_____

Fantasy

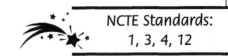

First Star on the Left

⭐ Objective:

Students will add illustrations or write details for events in a fantasy setting.

⭐ Materials:

- ★ *Harvey Potter's Balloon Farm* by Jerdine Holen Harold
- ★ One copy of "Strange Things Can Happen Here" for each student
- ★ Art paper, crayons, and colored pencils

⭐ Discussion:

The setting of a story is when and where it takes place.

The setting for a fantasy story can be a completely make-believe place, like

. . . a land where marshmallows grow on bushes,

. . . a planet where people have wings and can fly, or

. . . underwater where mermaids live and fish can talk.

What settings for stories do you know that aren't real?

(If students have trouble thinking of ideas, suggest stories with fantasy settings they would know, like *Where the Wild Things Are* or *Peter Pan*.)

⭐ Activity:

Read *Harvey Potter's Balloon Farm* to the group.

What parts of the setting in this story are real?

What parts of the setting are not real?

Have students complete the activity, "Strange Things Can Happen Here."

Ask students to read the events or show their drawings to the group and explain what is happening.

Display students' papers for all to enjoy.

Strange Things Can Happen Here

Draw or write three things that could happen in a fantasy story in this setting.

Fantasy

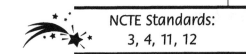
Characters, Setting, and Plot

⭐ Objectives:

Students will create a setting and characters for a fantasy story, then write a short story.

⭐ Materials:

- ★ *Happy Birthday, Dear Duck* by Eve Bunting
- ★ Display of student drawings of fantasy characters from the activity "Is Dear Duck a Real Duck?"
- ★ Selection of fantasy books (See the bibliography at the end of this section for suggestions.)
- ★ Art paper, crayons, and colored pencils
- ★ Lined paper and pencils

⭐ Discussion:

Stories have characters, settings, and plots.

   Who was the main character in *Happy Birthday, Dear Duck*?

   What was the setting for this book?

The plot includes events that take place in a story.

All stories have a beginning, a middle, and an ending.

   What happened at the beginning of *Happy Birthday, Dear Duck*?

   What happened in the middle of the story?

   How did the story end?

⭐ Activity:

Assign students to work in pairs. Ask them to talk with their partners about ideas for a setting and a character for a fantasy story.

They can work together on one drawing or do individual illustrations.

Students who are older can work together to write a short story about their setting and characters. Younger students can dictate their stories while an adults writes it.

If possible, type and print student stories on the computer.

Display the stories with the drawings for everyone to enjoy.

Select several of the student's stories to read during storytime.

Suggested Pairings of Nonfiction and Fantasy Books

Bats by Lynn M. Stone or *Squeaking Bats* by Ruth Berman and *Stellaluna* by Janell Cannon

Chickens by Peter Brady and *Hilda Hen's Scary Night* by Mary Wormell

Cows by Peter Brady and *When Bluebell Sang* by Lisa Campbell Ernst or *When Minnie and Moo Go Dancing* by Denys Cazet

Ducking Days by Karen Wallace and *Happy Birthday, Dear Duck* by Eve Bunting

Fishing Bears by Ruth Berman and *Good Job, Little Bear!* by Martin Waddell

Pigs by Peter Brady and *Oink* by Arthur Geisert

Sheep by Peter Brady and *Sheep in a Jeep* by Nancy Shaw

Ten Things I Know About Penguins by Wendy Wax and Della Rowland and *Tacky in Trouble* by Helen Lester

More Fantasy Books

Carle, Eric, *The Grouchy Ladybug.* HarperCollins, 1996.

Harold, Jerdine Nolen, *Harvey Potter's Balloon Farm.* Lothrop, Lee & Shepard, 1993.

Kraft, Erik, *Chocolatina.* BridgeWater, 1998.

Lester, Helen, *Tacky in Trouble.* Houghton Mifflin, 1998.

Loredo, Elizabeth, *Boogie Bones.* Putnam, 1997.

Marshall, James, *George and Martha.* Houghton Mifflin, 1972.

Meddaugh, Susan, *Martha Speaks.* Houghton Mifflin, 1992.

Nicole-Lisa, W., *Shake Dem Halloween Bones.* Houghton Mifflin, 1997.

Pilkey, Dav, *The Hallo-Weiner.* Blue Sky Press, 1995.

Pinkwater, Daniel M., *Young Larry.* Marshall Cavendish, 1997.

Schwartz, Alvin, *In a Dark, Dark Room and Other Scary Tales.* HarperCollins, 1984.

Sendak, Maurice, *Where the Wild Things Are.* HarperCollins, 1984.

Seuss, Dr., *And to Think That I Saw It on Mulberry Street.* Vanguard, 1937.

Turkle, Brinton, *Do Not Open.* Dutton, 1981.

Wells, Rosemary, *Bunny Cakes.* Dial, 1997

Historical Fiction

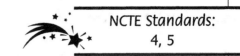

A Mix of Fact and Fiction

⭐ Objective:

Students will show an understanding of the chronological order of history and familiarize themselves with such terms as *before* and *after*, and *past, present,* and *future.*

⭐ Materials:

★ Photocopies of 4–6 illustrations from any book listed in the Historical Fiction Bibliography prepared to use on a flannel board

⭐ Discussion:

What does history mean? What does fiction mean?

Some stories are called historical fiction.

What do you think historical fiction means?

Would the setting for a historical fiction story be past, present, or future? Why?

The characters in a historical fiction story can be real people, like Abraham Lincoln or Martin Luther King.

Who else could be a character in a historical fiction story?

Even if the story is about real people, the author could add other characters that aren't real and details that are made up. That's what makes it fiction.

In a historical fiction story, the author includes details about the way things were at that time. If something wasn't invented yet, it can't be in the story.

⭐ Activity:

Place the photocopies in random order on the flannel board. Begin a discussion with your students about the logical sequence of the illustrations, rearranging them as your discussion progresses. Use sequencing words like *before, after,* etc.

Be prepared to discuss certain information about the illustrations. Young children will be interested in a discussion about why the characters are dressed differently, why their homes are different, or the kinds of activities the characters are participating in.

Read the story with the children. Discuss how your predicted sequencing varied from the actual story (if it did). Discuss which events in the story were "real" (history) and which were "made up" (fiction).

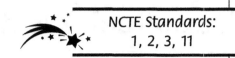

Time Traveler

⭐ Objective:

Students will evaluate advantages and disadvantages of living during the gold rush.

⭐ Materials:

★ *The Legend of Freedom Hill* by Linda Jacobs Altman

⭐ Activity:

Remind students that historical fiction is a story told during another time in history, based on facts, but also partly fiction.

Read *The Legend of Freedom Hill* to the group.

On the board, write two headings:

Good   Not so good

Ask students to name things they learned from the story that would be good about having lived in the West during the California gold rush. (Ideas might include: children had more freedom to go out, anyone could strike it rich, friendships were close, families were close.)

List their ideas in the "Good" column.

Then ask what might not have been so great about living at that time.

List their ideas in the "Not so good" column. (Ideas might include: slavery still existed, people were discriminated against on the basis of race and religion, no pizza, no computers.)

Ask students to vote:

How many of you would have liked to live at that time?

How many of you would not have liked to live then?

Ask for several volunteers from both sides to tell why they would or would not have liked to live then.

⭐ Extension:

Continue this activity by writing "Same" and "Different" in two columns and asking students for suggestions about how life then was similar and how it was different than today.

Historical Fiction Books

indicates those appropriate for older students

Altman, Linda Jacobs, *The Legend of Freedom Hill*. Lee & Low, 2000.

*Bunting, Eve, *The Blue and the Gray*. Scholastic, 1996.

Corey, Shana, *You Forgot Your Skirt, Amelia Bloomer!*: A Very Improper Story. Scholastic, 2000.

Hearne, Betsy, *Seven Brave Women*. Greenwillow, 1997.

Hopkinson, Deborah, *Sweet Clara and the Freedom Quilt*. Knopf, 1993.

Johnston, Tony, *The Quilt Story*. Putnam, 1985.

Kirkpatrick, Katherine, *Redcoats and Petticoats*. Holiday House, 1999.

Lorbiecki, Mary Beth, *Sister Anne's Hands*. Dial, 1998.

McCully, Emily Arnold, *Popcorn at the Palace*. Harcourt Brace, 1997.

*Nerlove, Miriam, *Flowers on the Wall*. Margaret K. Elderberry, 1996.

*Pollacco, Patricia, *Pink and Say*. Philomel, 1994.

Shea, Pegi Deitz, *The Whispering Cloth*. Boyds Mills, 1995.

Stanley, Diane, *Saving Sweetness*. Putnam, 1996.

Woodruff, Elvira, *The Memory Coat*. Scholastic, 1999.

*Yolen, Jane, *Encounter*. Harcourt Brace, 1992.

Nonfiction

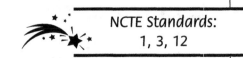

Fact or Fiction?

⚡ **Objective:**

Students will distinguish between fiction and nonfiction books.

⚡ **Materials:**

★ Several pairs of books from the suggested pairings of fiction and nonfiction bibliography at the end of this section

⚡ **Preparation:**

Select one fiction book and one nonfiction book on a topic the class is currently studying.

⚡ **Discussion:**

What does **fiction** mean?

What does **nonfiction** mean?

A nonfiction book is one that gives facts—true information about a subject.

⚡ **Activity:**

Read the following statements. Ask students to decide if they are fact or fiction.

Last summer I took a trip to (name a place you visited).

Next summer I plan to spend a week on the Moon.

When I was very young, I had a pet dinosaur.

Dinosaurs lived millions of years ago.

Last night I dreamed that I could fly.

(Students should understand that this statement is a fact: You had a dream, even though what happened is the dream was fiction.)

Ask several students to make statements. Let the rest of the class determine whether the statements are fact or fiction.

Read one fiction and nonfiction book on the same subject to the group. When you finish reading each book, ask students to state whether it was fiction or nonfiction.

Ask: What clues from the book did you use?

After reading the nonfiction book, ask students to name several facts they learned.

Provide a selection books. Ask students to work together to divide them into two piles: fiction and nonfiction.

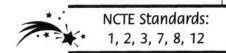

Just the Facts

⭐ Objective:

Students will use nonfiction books to prepare a report on an animal.

⭐ Materials:

One copy of the animal report reproducible for each student

⭐ Discussion:

Why do people write nonfiction books?

Why do people read nonfiction books?

If you wanted to learn more about different types of whales, should you read a fiction book or a nonfiction book?

If you wanted to learn how to make a puppet from a lunch bag or build a birdhouse, should you read a fiction or nonfiction book?

If you wanted to learn more about the Land of Oz or Never Never Land where Peter Pan lived, should you read a fiction or nonfiction book?

What kinds of things could you learn about snakes in a nonfiction book? (different types, where they live, what they eat, how big they are, etc.)

⭐ Activity:

Ask each student to decide on an animal he or she would like to learn more about. Younger children can work together in pairs.

Help each student find three nonfiction books on the animal he or she selected. The librarian can show students how to use the computer catalog and where to find the nonfiction section on animals.

A list of nonfiction books suitable for students this age can be found at the end of this section.

Student research can also be done on the Internet, but it is advisable to work one-on-one with children this age and to find and bookmark appropriate sites in advance.

Encourage students to add illustrations to their reports by drawing their own pictures, downloading pictures from the Internet, or photocopying pictures from nonfiction books.

Animal Report

 My animal

_____

 Where it lives

_____

_____

What it looks like

_____

_____

_____

What it eats

_____

_____

Animal Report (continued)

What I learned

_____

_____

_____

_____

Draw a picture of your animal in the box.

Bibliography

Suggested Pairings of Fiction and Nonfiction Books

Coming to America by Betsy Maestro (Scholastic, 1996) and *When Jessie Came Across the Sea* by Amy Hest (Candlewick, 1997)

Elmer by David McKee (Lothrop, 1989), *Elephants* by Claire Robinson (Heinemann Library, 1997), "The Elephant" in *Cats and Bats and Things with Wings* by Conrad Aiken (Atheneum, 1966), and "The Handiest Nose" by Aileen Fisher in *Side by Side: Poems to Read Together* collected by Lee Bennett Hopkins (Simon & Schuster, 1988)

Farming by Gail Gibbons (Holiday House, 1988) and *The Day Jimmy's Boa Ate the Wash* by Trina Hakes Noble (Dial, 1984, 1980)

From Caterpillar to Butterfly by Deborah Heiligman (Harper Trophy, 1996) and *The Very Hungry Caterpillar* by Eric Carle (Putman Publishing, 1983)

Going to the Hospital by Fred Rogers (Putnam, 1988) and *Franklin Goes to the Hospital* by Paulette Bourgeois (Kids Can, 2000)

Man on the Moon by Anastasia Suen (Viking, 1997) and *Zoom! Zoom! Zoom! I'm Off to the Moon* by Dan Yaccarino (Scholastic, 1997)

My Visit to the Zoo by Aliki (HarperCollins, 1997) and *If Anything Ever Goes Wrong at the Zoo* by Mary Jean Hendrick (Harcourt Brace, 1993)

Ten Things I Know About Penguins by Wendy Wax and Della Rowland (Contemporary, 1989) and *Tacky in Trouble* by Helen Lester (Houghton Mifflin, 1998)

To Be a Slave by Julius Lester (Dial, 1998) and *Journey to Freedom* by Courtni Wright (Holiday House, 1994)

Tyrannosaurus Rex by David Petersen (Childrens, 1989) and *Tyrone the Terrible* by Hans Wilhelm (Scholastic, 1988)

Nonfiction Books Grouped by Topic

Bakers by Tami Deedrick (Capstone, 1998).

Unbeatable Bread by Lyn Littlefield Hoopes (Dial, 1996).

All About Rattlesnakes by Jim Arnosky (Scholastic, 1997).

Soft Child: How Rattlesnake Got its Fangs by Joe Hayes (Rinehart, 1993).

Cats by Gail Gibbons (Holiday House, 1996).

Ginger by Charlotte Voake (Candlewick, 1997).

Dogs by Gerald Hawksley (Children's Press, 1989).

Dogs by Pam Jameson (Rourke Publications, 1989).

Big Moon Tortilla by Joy Cowley (Boyds Mills, 1998).

Tortilla Factory by Gary Paulsen (Harcourt Brace, 1995).

A Day in the Life of a Cowboy by Alvin G. Davis (Troll, 1991).

Cowboy Country by Ann Herbert Scott (Clarion, 1993).

Tyrannosaurus Rex by Elaine Landau (Children's Press, 1999).

What Happened to the Dinosaurs? by Franklyn M. Branley (Crowell, 1989).

The Lion Family Book by Angelika Hofer (Picture Book Studio, 1988).

Young Lions by Tuoshi Yoshida (Philomel Books, 1989).

Hurricanes by Arlene Erlbach (Children's Press, 1993).

Hurricanes by D.M. Sousa (Carolrhoda, 1996).

Storms by Ray Broekel (Children's Press, 1982).

Johnny Appleseed by Steven Kellogg (Morrow, 1988).

The Story of Johnny Appleseed by Aliki (Prentice Hall, 1963).

Hungry, Hungry Sharks by Joanna Cole (Random, 1986).

Sea Lions by Caroline Arnold (Morrow Junior Books, 1994).

Sharks by Gail Gibbons (Holiday House, 1992).

Sharks, Sharks, Sharks by Tina Anton (Raintree, 1989).

Splash!: A Book about Whales and Dolphins by Melvin Berger (Cartwheel Books, 2001).

The Great White Man-Eating Shark by Margaret Mahy (Dial, 1990).

What's It Like to be a Fish? by Wendy Pfeffer (Harper Trophy, 1996).

Contemporary Realism Picture Books

Barber, Barbara E., *Allie's Basketball Dream*. Lee & Low, 1996.

Bunting, Eve, *Smoky Night*. Harcourt, 1994.

Bunting, Eve, *Your Move*. Harcourt Brace, 1998.

Cowley, Joy, *Big Moon Tortilla*. Boyds Mills, 1998.

Grimes, Nikki, *My Man Blue*. Dial, 1999.

Haller, Danita, *Not Just Any Ring*. Knopf, 1982.

Hoffman, Mary, *Amazing Grace*. Dial, 1991.

Polacco, Patricia, *My Rotten Redheaded Brother*. Simon & Schuster, 1994.

Raczek, Linda Theresa, *The Night the Grandfathers Danced*. Northland, 1995.

Raczek, Linda Theresa, *Rainy's Pow Wow*. Rising Moon, 1999.

Scott, Ann Herbert, *Brave as a Mountain Lion*. Clarion, 1996.

Sharmat, Marjorie Weinman, *Gila Monsters Meet You at the Airport*. Scott Foresman, 1983.

Soto, Gary, *Too Many Tamales*. Putnam, 1996.

Mysteries for Beginners

Adler, David A., *Young Cam Jansen and the Dinosaur Game*. Viking, 1996.

Platt, Kin, *Big Max in the Mystery of the Missing Moose*. Harper & Row, 1977.

Sharmat, Marjorie Weinman, *Nate the Great and the Lost List*. Coward, McCann, 1975.

Yolen, Jane, *Picnic with Piggins*. Harcourt Brace, 1988.

Science Fiction: Easy Readers and Picture Books

Layton, Neal, *Smile If You're Human*. Dial, 1999.

McPhail, David, *Tinker and Tom and the Star Baby*. Little, Brown, 1998.

Siracusa, Catherine, *The Banana Split from Outer Space*. Hyperion, 1995.

Weisner, David, *June 29, 1999*. Clarion, 1992.

Willis, Jeanne, *The Long Blue Blazer*. Dutton, 1987.

Yaccarino, Dan, *Zoom! Zoom! Zoom! I'm Off to the Moon!* Scholastic, 1997.

Yolen, Jane, *Commander Toad and the Planet of the Grapes*. Coward McCann, 1982.

Printed in the USA
CPSIA information can be obtained
at www.ICGtesting.com
LVHW080723170724
785510LV00007B/276